LIFE ALONG THE WAY SERIES
BY JOURNEY**WISE**

A 90-DAY DEVOTIONAL

JESUS
THROUGH US

FOLLOWING HIS EXAMPLE
IN LOVE AND SERVICE

FOREWORD BY
SHANE STANFORD

WHITAKER
HOUSE

JESUS THROUGH US:
Following His Example in Love and Service

JourneyWise
PO Box 382662
Germantown, TN 38183
https://journeywise.network/

ISBN: 979-8-88769-086-5
eBook ISBN: 979-8-88769-087-2
Printed in the United States of America
© 2024 by The Moore-West Center for Disciple Formation

Whitaker House
1030 Hunt Valley Circle
New Kensington, PA 15068
www.whitakerhouse.com

Library of Congress Control Number: 2024930177

1 2 3 4 5 6 7 8 9 10 11 ⨆ 31 30 29 28 27 26 25 24

CONTENTS

FOREWORD

Jesus replied: "'Love the Lord your God with all your heart and with all your soul and with all your mind.' This the first and greatest commandment. And the second is like it: 'Love your neighbor as yourself.'" Matthew 22:37–39 NIV

In *Jesus Among Us*—the second leg of the Life Along the Way Series—we saw how God unveiled the person of Jesus Christ as One who is both fully human and fully divine. At that intersection, Jesus's journey on earth was one of miracles and amazing events angled into the everyday lives of people. Jesus living among others, with their problems, struggles, concerns, and even their normal, ordinary experiences—it all meant something more. It meant that not only was Jesus in their midst, but *God the Father* was too. Jesus's presence elevates the nature of the "everyday" into crucial intersections for God to know and be known, and for the world to be changed forever. The fact that Jesus was among us transformed everything.

In this third leg of the series, *Jesus Through Us*, as we progress on our one-year journey with Jesus, we learn about the impact of His love and grace. It is a continuation of the great revelation of God's presence with creation. He is with us, He is among us, and He works through us in our daily lives. In this intimate devotional, we explore additional interactions Jesus had with people along the way, including those in need of miracles, those in search of inclusion into the family, and many simply craving the basic need for care and touch. But we also begin to see the power of our part in the journey. To align our lives with the life of Jesus means we are invested in the lives of others. We become Christ in their path. As we make this journey, we learn more about Jesus, but we also learn about ourselves and the role we play in sharing the hope of Christ by loving like Jesus in the world.

Thus, in this portion of our exploration into Jesus's life, as we see the importance of experiencing His teachings, interactions, and love, of settling in and allowing our sense of awe to transform into practical lessons for each day, we become more than just fellow travelers—we become Jesus's hands and feet. As we have noted, in the first-century church, travel required substantial effort and planning. The time spent traveling afforded not only a *deeper* picture of the world, but a *bigger* picture as well, enabling people to come to a better understanding of purpose, development, and destination. We have the privilege of traveling through life with the greatest Teacher, Friend, and Savior we could ever know. He invites you, at any point in your journey, to ask the questions that lie deep in your soul, and to spend time pondering how your answers fit within the context of His life and words and example.

As with any trip, to arrive at your desired destination, you must remain faithful and consistent. Yes, each leg of the journey starts with the first step, but it continues with the next step and the next, putting one foot in front of the other and never giving up. If you want to finish well, the next step you take—the next commitment, the next act of faithfulness—matters. Don't give up, but give in to where the road leads. Give in to what the narrative asks from each of us. By looking at the life and ministry of Jesus, we discover what it means to actually follow Him.

To walk with Jesus through His earthly life—as a friend and fellow traveler on the road—is to witness a holy God enter into humanity's journey and make it His own in order to redeem us and give us true life. Where are you in your journey with Jesus? As we have mentioned from the start, to meet Him at the beginning is a divine discovery, but to set out on the road with Him as He teaches, heals, and guides us in His love is powerful, personal, and full of purpose that we can carry into every day. Now we are called to do something with what we know and have experienced from Jesus. We might disavow Him, sure, but we cannot ignore Him. As you travel through this devotional, I encourage you to reflect further on the humanity of Jesus's earthly journey. Listen to His conversations with family members and friends. Hear the Father give Him His next directions and destinations. Watch the equally human and divine story of Jesus unfold before your eyes. I pray that by doing so, you will find yourself walking ever more closely with the One who is always with us, among us, and working through us.

—*Shane Stanford*
Founder and CEO, The Moore-West Center for Applied Theology
President, JourneyWise

FOLLOWING JESUS IN LOVE AND SERVICE

If you've journeyed with us for books one and two of the Life Along the Way series, you're familiar with the heart and approach behind these devotionals. But, if not, starting here at book three, *Jesus Through Us*, is still a great launching point for the journey!

We created the four Life Along the Way daily devotionals to capture the essence of Jesus's life, ministry, death, and ascension, to follow the example that Jesus left in the Gospels, and to encourage us all to invite Him into our journey each day.

We believe that every one of us is on a journey through life. Each day, each interaction is an opportunity for us to either learn and grow in Jesus or to become more entrenched in the things this world offers. In other words, each day is an opportunity to focus on loving and serving others better or to put our focus merely on our careers, the things we want to do and buy, and our personal goals and desires.

In *Jesus Through Us*, we will look at the example of Jesus's outward ministry—the way He loved, the way He served, the way He *saw* the people around Him and cared for them in the most beautiful, life-giving way—and how His example should impact our own lives. As you progress through this devotional, you will be an eyewitness as Jesus multiplies His ministry by sending out His disciples, challenges His followers to serve God and others wholeheartedly, heals lepers, raises Lazarus from the dead, faces plots against His life, and rides triumphantly as King into Jerusalem, where He speaks of the resurrection of believers just before His own death and resurrection.

Jesus modeled a life of sacrifice and "otherness." He lived every day focused on the people around Him and the mission He was given. For those who have an ear to hear, God desires that we follow in Jesus's footsteps in this way. Not only did God leave us instructions in the Bible for how to do this, but His Son, Jesus, wants to journey *alongside* us as we travel this road.

If you're new to this series, we want you to know that each devotional is designed to be read in ninety days, but you can just as easily go at your own pace. It's okay if you get behind or if you read ahead or if you move through the books out of order. (While we encourage you to read the books sequentially, you may read them in any order you choose.) It's okay if it takes you a year to go through each book. The idea is that you're getting to know the journey of Jesus and allowing His journey to shape and direct yours.

The four Life Along the Way books are as follows:

1. *Jesus with Us: Meeting Him Where He Began*

2. *Jesus Among Us: Walking with Him in His Ministry and Miracles*

3. *Jesus Through Us: Following His Example in Love and Service*

4. *Jesus in Us: Living Wholeheartedly the Life He Intends*

Whether you've been in the church your whole life, are a curious skeptic, or find yourself somewhere in between, we hope that this journey through Scripture focused on the way Jesus "did life" will add great purpose to your *Life Along the Way*. We trust that God will give you wisdom for the journey as He grows you into His likeness, that you will be transformed as you live daily with Jesus, and that this study will be key in helping you to live every day as Jesus would.

Second Peter 1:5–7 says, "*Make every effort to add to your faith goodness; and to goodness, knowledge; and to knowledge, self-control; and to self-control, perseverance; and to perseverance, godliness; and to godliness, mutual affection; and to mutual affection, love*" (NIV).

Experiencing life with Jesus will lead you to become more deeply committed to God and to serving others in His name. As you journey with Jesus, our hope is that you would *love Jesus* and *love like Jesus*.

Let's keep traveling the road!

—*The JourneyWise Team*

DAY 1:
USING WHAT WE ARE

SCRIPTURE READING

JOHN 9:1–11 (NLT)

As Jesus was walking along, he saw a man who had been blind from birth. "Rabbi," his disciples asked him, "why was this man born blind? Was it because of his own sins or his parents' sins?"

"It was not because of his sins or his parents' sins," Jesus answered. "This happened so the power of God could be seen in him. We must quickly carry out the tasks assigned us by the one who sent us. The night is coming, and then no one can work. But while I am here in the world, I am the light of the world."

Then he spit on the ground, made mud with the saliva, and spread the mud over the blind man's eyes. He told him, "Go wash yourself in the pool of Siloam" (Siloam means "sent"). So the man went and washed and came back seeing!

His neighbors and others who knew him as a blind beggar asked each other, "Isn't this the man who used to sit and beg?" Some said he was, and others said, "No, he just looks like him!"

But the beggar kept saying, "Yes, I am the same one!"

They asked, "Who healed you? What happened?"

He told them, "The man they call Jesus made mud and spread it over my eyes and told me, 'Go to the pool of Siloam and wash yourself.' So I went and washed, and now I can see!"

LIFE LESSONS

When we hit a rough point in our life or watch something bad happen to someone else, it can be easy to wonder if we're being punished in some way. We receive a bad diagnosis, and we ponder whether we did something wrong. We wind up in a car accident and assume that God is mad at us. We get demoted and wonder if God had something to do with it. Sound familiar?

Although our actions do have consequences, suffering isn't always related to our life choices. It's part of the human experience and can hit without regard to what's fair, how wonderful or awful we've been, or what we've done. And some of us end up with rougher storms to weather than others.

Jesus healed blind men several times over the course of His time on earth, but the account in John 9 is unique. This is the only time in Scripture when Jesus healed a man *"blind from birth"* (verse 1). This phrase in Greek is found nowhere else in the New Testament. The disciples assumed the man had been born blind because of his own sin or the sin of his parents, but Jesus quashed that assumption immediately, saying it happened *"so the power of God could be seen in him"* (verse 3).

We are all subject to a broken world, sinners by nature, and spiritually blind from birth. God uses what we are, though, and He offers us hope and forgiveness and demonstrates His power through our lives. He offers healing and comfort when it feels like we're drudging through an impossible situation. And He gradually opens our eyes to truly see Him.

WHERE ARE YOU?

When has God opened your eyes to see Him more clearly during a hard situation?

What do you think about this statement of Jesus in John 9:3: "This happened so the power of God could be seen in him"?

How has your life displayed the power of God in the world?

_____

_____

_____

_____

_____

A PRAYER

Jesus, thank You for opening blinded eyes, both physically and spiritually. Give me eyes that see You more clearly each day. Please help me through whatever comes my way, even when it seems impossible, so the world may see Your power in my life. In Your name, amen.

DAY 2:
WHEN THE WORLD WALKS OUT

SCRIPTURE READING

JOHN 9:12–34 (NLT)

"Where is he now?" they asked.

"I don't know," he replied.

Then they took the man who had been blind to the Pharisees, because it was on the Sabbath that Jesus had made the mud and healed him. The Pharisees asked the man all about it. So he told them, "He put the mud over my eyes, and when I washed it away, I could see!"

Some of the Pharisees said, "This man Jesus is not from God, for he is working on the Sabbath." Others said, "But how could an ordinary sinner do such miraculous signs?" So there was a deep division of opinion among them.

Then the Pharisees again questioned the man who had been blind and demanded, "What's your opinion about this man who healed you?"

The man replied, "I think he must be a prophet."

The Jewish leaders still refused to believe the man had been blind and could now see, so they called in his parents. They asked them, "Is this your son? Was he born blind? If so, how can he now see?"

His parents replied, "We know this is our son and that he was born blind, but we don't know how he can see or who healed him. Ask him. He is old enough to speak for himself." His parents said this because they were afraid of the Jewish leaders, who had announced that anyone saying Jesus was the Messiah would be expelled from the synagogue. That's why they said, "He is old enough. Ask him."

So for the second time they called in the man who had been blind and told him, "God should get the glory for this, because we know this man Jesus is a sinner."

"I don't know whether he is a sinner," the man replied. "But I know this: I was blind, and now I can see!"

"But what did he do?" they asked. "How did he heal you?"

"Look!" the man exclaimed. "I told you once. Didn't you listen? Why do you want to hear it again? Do you want to become his disciples, too?"

Then they cursed him and said, "You are his disciple, but we are disciples of Moses! We know God spoke to Moses, but we don't even know where this man comes from."

"Why, that's very strange!" the man replied. "He healed my eyes, and yet you don't know where he comes from? We know that God doesn't listen to sinners, but he is ready to hear those who worship him and do his will. Ever since the world began, no one has been able to open the eyes of someone born blind. If this man were not from God, he couldn't have done it."

"You were born a total sinner!" they answered. "Are you trying to teach us?" And they threw him out of the synagogue.

LIFE LESSONS

It's hard to deny a miracle that's standing right in front of you. But as we see in this passage from John, it's absolutely possible to try. People saw this man they knew had been blind from birth now seeing clearly—but instead of celebrating the miracle he experienced, they questioned its validity. The Pharisees asked the man who had healed him. Then they asked his parents if he had really been born blind. After this, they *again* asked the man how he had been healed—they just had to double-check. The village should have been throwing the man a celebration. Instead, all he got was confrontation and insults.

Sometimes when Jesus walks into your life, the world walks out. And it might even try to take you with it. Holding fast to what you know to be true can be a struggle—especially when people try to discredit you or drag you down. Hold tight! Just because someone else can't see the truth does not mean you should close your eyes again. Keep your own encounters with Jesus at the forefront of your mind. It's much better to walk with Him than to wander blindly with the crowd.

WHERE ARE YOU?

Why are the Pharisees so upset here?

_____

_____

_____

_____

_____

Has anyone ever confronted you about your faith? What happened?

_____

_____

_____

_____

_____

How can you keep your eyes open when people around you want to keep theirs firmly shut?

_____

_____

_____

_____

_____

A PRAYER

Lord, I pray for You to continue transforming my life and opening my eyes to You. Help me to keep my patience when I'm confronted with questions about my faith. Help me to always remember my personal encounters with You so I can hold fast to them when the world tempts me to doubt. In Your name, amen.

DAY 3:
CHOOSING BLINDNESS

SCRIPTURE READING

JOHN 9:35–41 (NLT)

When Jesus heard what had happened, he found the man and asked, "Do you believe in the Son of Man?"

The man answered, "Who is he, sir? I want to believe in him."

"You have seen him," Jesus said, "and he is speaking to you!"

"Yes, Lord, I believe!" the man said. And he worshiped Jesus.

Then Jesus told him, "I entered this world to render judgment—to give sight to the blind and to show those who think they see that they are blind."

Some Pharisees who were standing nearby heard him and asked, "Are you saying we're blind?"

"If you were blind, you wouldn't be guilty," Jesus replied. "But you remain guilty because you claim you can see."

LIFE LESSONS

Nobody likes change. And when that change reveals that we've been wrong all along, it's a hard pill to swallow. So hard, in fact, that many people would rather blindly cling to their misguided beliefs than open their eyes to the new truth that's been revealed to them. But wandering around with our eyes shut, refusing to let go of what we knew and open ourselves to something new, prevents us from moving forward. It's like wandering around with our hands over our eyes, insisting we know exactly where we're going.

The Pharisees considered themselves high up on the charts in regard to moral and spiritual understanding. The idea that they could be blind to higher knowledge, to understanding, and to God Himself must have seemed ridiculous to them! Surely, they were too smart, too knowledgeable, for that. Yet each time they encountered Jesus, they failed to truly see Him and the truth in front of them. They catered to their religion over the physical proof, choosing to close their eyes so that they could hold on to their previous, familiar beliefs.

When we're not receptive to new truths, we can find ourselves choosing preset religion over new understanding. This happens when we're afraid to be wrong or want to feel like we've got it all figured out. But this just stalls our progress toward Jesus. Instead, we must be brave enough to open our eyes, admit that even our longest-held convictions may be incorrect, and allow Jesus to move in our lives.

WHERE ARE YOU?

How is it possible for people to know all about Jesus but still be spiritually blind?

_____

_____

_____

_____

_____

Have you ever shut your eyes to something you knew might be true because it meant admitting you were wrong?

_____

_____

_____

_____

A PRAYER

Jesus, please help me not to be blinded by religion or my own opinions. I don't want my pride to block my growth. Help me to trust in who You are. Open my eyes to see the things I don't yet know about You. In Your name, amen.

DAY 4:
THE GATE AND THE GOOD SHEPHERD

SCRIPTURE READING

JOHN 10:1–21 (MSG)

"Let me set this before you as plainly as I can. If a person climbs over or through the fence of a sheep pen instead of going through the gate, you know he's up to no good—a sheep rustler! The shepherd walks right up to the gate. The gatekeeper opens the gate to him and the sheep recognize his voice. He calls his own sheep by name and leads them out. When he gets them all out, he leads them and they follow because they are familiar with his voice. They won't follow a stranger's voice but will scatter because they aren't used to the sound of it."

Jesus told this simple story, but they had no idea what he was talking about. So he tried again. "I'll be explicit, then. I am the Gate for the sheep. All those others are up to no good—sheep rustlers, every one of them. But the sheep didn't listen to them. I am the Gate. Anyone who goes through me will be cared for—will freely go in and out, and find pasture. A thief is only there to steal and kill and destroy. I came so they can have real and eternal life, more and better life than they ever dreamed of.

"I am the Good Shepherd. The Good Shepherd puts the sheep before himself, sacrifices himself if necessary. A hired man is not a real shepherd. The sheep mean nothing to him. He sees a wolf come and runs for it, leaving the sheep to be ravaged and scattered by the wolf. He's only in it for the money. The sheep don't matter to him.

"I am the Good Shepherd. I know my own sheep and my own sheep know me. In the same way, the Father knows me and I know the Father. I put the sheep before myself, sacrificing myself if necessary. You need to know that I have other sheep in addition to those in this pen. I need to gather and bring them, too. They'll also recognize my voice. Then it will be one flock, one Shepherd. This is why the Father loves me: because I freely lay down my life. And so I am free to take it up again. No one takes it from me. I lay it down of my own free will. I have the right to lay it down; I also have the right to take it up again. I received this authority personally from my Father."

This kind of talk caused another split in the Jewish ranks. A lot of them were saying, "He's crazy, a maniac—out of his head completely. Why bother listening to him?" But others weren't so sure: "These aren't the words of a crazy man. Can a 'maniac' open blind eyes?"

LIFE LESSONS

Many of us long to be in charge, but not everybody is cut out to be a leader. Often, we find ourselves drawn to the superficial aspects of leadership, mesmerized by visions of people respecting us, admiring us, listening to us, and following our instructions without question. But, throughout Scripture, Jesus paints a picture of leadership that is a lot less glamorous: someone willing to set aside their own needs and well-being to care for their followers—even to the point of sacrificing themselves.

In biblical times, shepherds would protect their sheep at night by putting them in a cave or a high-walled pen made of boulders. Then the shepherd would position himself in front of the enclosure's only entrance. This meant that a predator seeking to attack the sheep would have to get past the shepherd first. A shepherd who cared for his own well-being over the sheep's might run at the first sign of real danger. But a good shepherd would protect the herd at all costs.

Jesus describes Himself here as the Gate and the Good Shepherd. He is the only way in or out, and He will do whatever it takes to keep His sheep safe in His care. Jesus accepted His position as our Shepherd and Savior knowing full well that doing so would require Him to sacrifice everything.

WHERE ARE YOU?

How has Jesus protected you from harm?

How does Jesus keep you safe from whatever might pull you away from Him?

_____

_____

_____

_____

_____

Take some time today to make a list of what makes Jesus the Good Shepherd.

_____

_____

_____

_____

_____

A PRAYER

Jesus, thank You for being the Gate for the sheep and the Good Shepherd. It's so good to know I'm safe in Your arms. I'm grateful for Your protection and Your willingness to make sacrifices for me. In Your name, amen.

DAY 5:
THE WORKER'S ROLE

SCRIPTURE READING

LUKE 10:1–12 (CEV)

Later the Lord chose 72 other followers and sent them out two by two to every town and village where he was about to go. He said to them:

> *A large crop is in the fields, but there are only a few workers. Ask the Lord in charge of the harvest to send out workers to bring it in. Now go, but remember, I am sending you like lambs into a pack of wolves. Don't take along a moneybag or a traveling bag or sandals. And don't waste time greeting people on the road. As soon as you enter a home, say, "God bless this home with peace." If the people living there are peace-loving, your prayer for peace will bless them. But if they are not peace-loving, your prayer will return to you. Stay with the same family, eating and drinking whatever they give you, because workers are worth what they earn. Don't move around from house to house.*
>
> *If the people of a town welcome you, eat whatever they offer. Heal their sick and say, "God's kingdom will soon be here!"*
>
> *But if the people of a town refuse to welcome you, go out into the street and say, "We are shaking the dust from our feet as a warning to you. And you can be sure that God's kingdom will soon be here!" I tell you that on the day of judgment the people of Sodom will get off easier than the people of that town!*

LIFE LESSONS

Being rejected is rough. Not knowing how you'll be received is draining. Wanting something better for someone and watching them turn it down can be soul-crushing. But as hard as those moments are, they do not mean that we've failed or let God down. Hopefully, Jesus's words in this passage take a great weight off your shoulders: *you are not in charge of the harvest.*

Only Christ has the power to save. You're needed out in the field to spread His love and message, but people's reactions and final decisions are not on you. Their ultimate choices are not your burden to bear. The choices that people make for or against God are not up to us. God just needs our willingness and our heart for Him, and then He is in charge of what happens from there. He will do the harvesting if His workers do the planting. And planting comes in all manner of ways.

So, live your life alongside God and keep your heart open and loving. Be an example. Listen for what He's asking of you and boldly step forward. Then, know that it's ultimately in His hands.

WHERE ARE YOU?

In what ways are you a worker for God right now, out in the world planting seeds?

_____

_____

_____

_____

_____

What more do you think God might be asking you to do?

_____

_____

_____

_____

_____

A PRAYER

Lord, help me to plant seeds in the way I live my life—under Your guidance, strength, and love. Help me to let go of the outcome and trust that You are in control. And please, send more workers to join me. Amen.

DAY 6:
THE REAL REJECTEE

SCRIPTURE READING

MATTHEW 11:20–24 (NIV)

Then Jesus began to denounce the towns in which most of his miracles had been performed, because they did not repent. "Woe to you, Chorazin! Woe to you, Bethsaida! For if the miracles that were performed in you had been performed in Tyre and Sidon, they would have repented long ago in sackcloth and ashes. But I tell you, it will be more bearable for Tyre and Sidon on the day of judgment than for you. And you, Capernaum, will you be lifted to the heavens? No, you will go down to Hades. For if the miracles that were performed in you had been performed in Sodom, it would have remained to this day. But I tell you that it will be more bearable for Sodom on the day of judgment than for you."

SEE ALSO: LUKE 10:13–16

LIFE LESSONS

Many people fear sharing their love for God because they fear rejection—and rejection can hit pretty hard and feel pretty rotten! But Jesus plainly emphasizes here that it's not you or me that the people are rejecting. They are rejecting Him.

Jesus mentioned two cities, Chorazin and Bethsaida, that refused God. The people in these cities had witnessed major miracles, and they had been exposed to Jesus's teachings. Yet, despite all of His words and wonders, they still *chose* to refuse Him. They'd seen and heard it all, but they still said, "No thanks." There was nothing more to be done.

Their refusal portrays their feelings about God; and, yes, there are consequences for ignoring God's call. But this is a key point to take to heart: *people rejected Jesus to His face.* He's the hope behind it all, and even He did not always win people's hearts.

It can be hard to remember all of this when someone is cruel toward us or lashes out at us. But know that it's all part of the job. Take a breath and don't stop loving those around you. Accept the choices of others with grace and good humor. Maybe it's not their time yet—and God can handle that.

WHERE ARE YOU?

What causes you to hesitate to talk to people about what you believe?

_____

_____

_____

_____

_____

Has someone ever reacted poorly to something you've said (especially something related to God)? What happened?

_____

_____

_____

_____

_____

If someone is cruel to you in response to your relationship with God, how can you continue to love them and not judge them?

_____

_____

_____

_____

_____

A PRAYER

God, please help me to not be afraid to talk about You with others. In the end, it's all about You, not me. Help me to keep caring for and loving those who are lost, even when they've been harsh or hurtful. Help me to rest in Your love and acceptance and continue extending them to others. In Your name, amen.

DAY 7:
CREDIT WHERE CREDIT IS DUE

SCRIPTURE READING

LUKE 10:17–20 (NIV)

The seventy-two returned with joy and said, "Lord, even the demons submit to us in your name."

He replied, "I saw Satan fall like lightning from heaven. I have given you authority to trample on snakes and scorpions and to overcome all the power of the enemy; nothing will harm you. However, do not rejoice that the spirits submit to you, but rejoice that your names are written in heaven."

LIFE LESSONS

Being connected to God can feel powerful. Conquering our insecurities and fears, gaining the courage to stand up for ourselves and others, gaining significant wisdom and knowledge—each of these areas of growth in our lives can make us feel nearly invincible. We should certainly find joy in these things and celebrate our victories (even the small ones), but let's pay attention to our focus after an achievement. Where are we giving credit? Who are we really celebrating? Are we worshipping the overcoming itself or the One who made it possible?

In this passage from Luke, Jesus's seventy-two followers seem mightily impressed by their newfound authority to cast out demons, but He is quick to remind them that He is the One who gave them that authority.

Relishing power and success over the grace of God can slip into our lives so easily, and once it's there, it can be hard to see and even harder to submit to God. As we grow in Christ, we will find a new way of life that brings with it a holy confidence, zeal, and authority, and these things can so easily become the object of our worship. We can't allow ourselves to forget, though, that the real reason to celebrate is God. The real secret to our new lives is the hope and goodness He brings. Sure, we might be out here putting in the work; but, ultimately, it's not about us—every result is from Him. It's only because He is working through us that we have newfound hope and assurance.

WHERE ARE YOU?

What was the last life event or achievement you celebrated?

_____
_____
_____
_____
_____

How did you celebrate?

_____
_____
_____
_____
_____

How was God evident in that event in your life?

_____
_____
_____
_____
_____

A PRAYER

Jesus, help me to always keep in mind that it's Your hand working in my life. Help me to give credit where credit is due. You are always there for me, helping me along, being there for me. Please don't let me fall into thinking I achieve anything by my own power. Help me to remember that You are the One working through me and empowering me. In Your name, amen.

DAY 8:
ADMITTING AND ACCEPTING

SCRIPTURE READING

MATTHEW 11:25–30 (NIV)

At that time Jesus said, "I praise you, Father, Lord of heaven and earth, because you have hidden these things from the wise and learned, and revealed them to little children. Yes, Father, for this is what you were pleased to do.

"All things have been committed to me by my Father. No one knows the Son except the Father, and no one knows the Father except the Son and those to whom the Son chooses to reveal him.

"Come to me, all you who are weary and burdened, and I will give you rest. Take my yoke upon you and learn from me, for I am gentle and humble in heart, and you will find rest for your souls. For my yoke is easy and my burden is light."

SEE ALSO: LUKE 10:21–24

LIFE LESSONS

Thinking that we know better than others is addicting. Being the so-called smartest person in the room has a certain allure that is hard to let go of. Yet believing that we alone are wise in the ways of this world can lead to a sense of self-importance, arrogance, and self-trust that doesn't permit the opinions of others or make room for new thoughts and ideas, and is, in turn, isolating.

Accepting Jesus means recognizing that you lack full understanding and need His wisdom. It means admitting you are not all-knowing, that you don't always understand, and that there is something greater than your thoughts and ideas.

Young children have a simple trust and deep dependence on their parents. It brings joy to Jesus's heart when His followers place this same childlike dependence on their heavenly Father. It brings Him joy to see them fully committed, accepting, laying down everything, setting aside their own plans, following even when they can't yet see everything that's down the line.

WHERE ARE YOU?

What does a "childlike faith" mean to you?

_____

_____

_____

_____

_____

In your own words, why does Jesus appreciate a childlike faith so much?

_____

_____

_____

_____

_____

What do you think it means that God "hid these things" from people who consider themselves wise and clever?

_____

_____

_____

_____

_____

A PRAYER

Father, give me childlike faith. Help me to trust more in You and Your plan for me. Don't let me fall into thinking I am too good or too smart for deeper understandings or new concepts. Help me to keep my mind and heart open. In Jesus's name, amen.

DAY 9:
LOVE ACROSS SOCIAL LINES

SCRIPTURE READING

LUKE 10:25–37 (NLT)

One day an expert in religious law stood up to test Jesus by asking him this question: "Teacher, what should I do to inherit eternal life?"

Jesus replied, "What does the law of Moses say? How do you read it?"

The man answered, "'You must love the Lord your God with all your heart, all your soul, all your strength, and all your mind.' And, 'Love your neighbor as yourself.'"

"Right!" Jesus told him. "Do this and you will live!"

The man wanted to justify his actions, so he asked Jesus, "And who is my neighbor?"

Jesus replied with a story: "A Jewish man was traveling from Jerusalem down to Jericho, and he was attacked by bandits. They stripped him of his clothes, beat him up, and left him half dead beside the road.

"By chance a priest came along. But when he saw the man lying there, he crossed to the other side of the road and passed him by. A Temple assistant walked over and looked at him lying there, but he also passed by on the other side.

"Then a despised Samaritan came along, and when he saw the man, he felt compassion for him. Going over to him, the Samaritan soothed his wounds with olive oil and wine and bandaged them. Then he put the man on his own donkey and took him to an inn, where he took care of him. The next day he handed the innkeeper two silver coins, telling him, 'Take care of this man. If his bill runs higher than this, I'll pay you the next time I'm here.'

"Now which of these three would you say was a neighbor to the man who was attacked by bandits?" Jesus asked.

The man replied, "The one who showed him mercy."

Then Jesus said, "Yes, now go and do the same."

LIFE LESSONS

Everything comes down to love. Loving God and loving others are the greatest commandments, and if you love God, you will obey His command to love others. But what does that mean, really?

Even this expert in the law wanted to hear Jesus's answer to this question. To illustrate what it means to actually live out the greatest commandments, Jesus told him the story of the Good Samaritan. In this story, the priest and the temple assistant knew the royal law, but they didn't live it out. The Samaritan, on the other hand, showed love to the man in need. He threw aside societal divisions and any thought of how he'd been treated himself, and he took the time to genuinely help this man.

The Samaritan is the example of how to obey God's greatest command. We give of ourselves, doing what we would hope others would do for us (and more) in that position. We leave judgment and hatred behind and approach others with tenderness and compassion.

WHERE ARE YOU?

Give a modern-day illustration of the story of the Good Samaritan.

_____

_____

_____

_____

_____

What would be your personal answer to the question in Luke 10:29: "Who is my neighbor?"

_____

_____

_____

_____

_____

How does God's love show up in how you treat others?

_____

_____

_____

_____

_____

When has it been hard for you to love your neighbor?

_____

_____

_____

_____

_____

A PRAYER

Jesus, help me to love others as much as You love me. Show me ways to demonstrate Your love to others. Give me Your deep compassion for the plights of other people. Help me realize that my neighbor is whoever has a need that I can meet. In Your name, amen.

DAY 10:
A PROPER PRIORITY CHECKLIST

SCRIPTURE READING

LUKE 10:38–42 (MSG)

As they continued their travel, Jesus entered a village. A woman by the name of Martha welcomed him and made him feel quite at home. She had a sister, Mary, who sat before the Master, hanging on every word he said. But Martha was pulled away by all she had to do in the kitchen. Later, she stepped in, interrupting them. "Master, don't you care that my sister has abandoned the kitchen to me? Tell her to lend me a hand."

The Master said, "Martha, dear Martha, you're fussing far too much and getting yourself worked up over nothing. One thing only is essential, and Mary has chosen it—it's the main course, and won't be taken from her."

LIFE LESSONS

Life can throw many distractions our way—and many of them are good! Yet even good things will consume our time and attention if we don't have our priorities set. We begin to feel like we *need* to do whatever-it-is *right now*: we *need* to spend our time in a certain way, we *need* to figure out a solution to a problem, we *need* to finish our very good to-do list. How often do we let the things we need to do to survive, to take care of our families, and even to serve God take over our time spent actually enjoying God?

Mary wanted to give Jesus a proper welcome. This was a good thing! But it took her focus off what really mattered: Jesus Himself. Her priority should have been Him. The house didn't need to be spotless. She didn't have to make a huge dinner. Everything didn't need to be just so. But she let her priorities get out of order when she chose to focus on those things. She chose preparing *around* Him instead of spending time *with* Him.

When you find yourself checking off those hundreds of tiny details—that one extra Bible study, that freshly made dinner instead of boxed, that one chapter a day you promised yourself you would read, that second charity walk—ask yourself if you're checking every box *other* than spending time with Christ.

WHERE ARE YOU?

What life details do you find yourself most distracted by?

_____
_____
_____
_____
_____

What expectations do you set for yourself on your walk with Christ that keep you from actually spending time with Him?

_____
_____
_____
_____
_____

What can you do differently to make sure you don't overlook spending time in God's presence?

_____
_____
_____
_____
_____

A PRAYER

Lord, help me to look past the distractions and keep my eyes focused on You. Give me the wisdom to slow down and prioritize what is most important and what truly benefits my walk with You. In Your name, amen.

DAY 11:
START SIMPLE

SCRIPTURE READING

LUKE 11:1–4 (NIV)

One day Jesus was praying in a certain place. When he finished, one of his disciples said to him, "Lord, teach us to pray, just as John taught his disciples."

He said to them, "When you pray, say:

> *"'Father,*
> *hallowed be your name,*
> *your kingdom come.*
> *Give us each day our daily bread.*
> *Forgive us our sins,*
> *for we also forgive everyone who sins against us.*
> *And lead us not into temptation.'"*

LIFE LESSONS

Prayer can seem daunting: you're talking to the Creator of the universe, asking for the things you want, feeling guilty over the things you think you *should* be asking for but aren't, trying to make your time with Him count in the best way possible. It almost sounds like an awkward date! A relationship with God takes work and practice, just like all of our relationships.

In their time with Jesus, the disciples heard Him pray to God numerous times, yet of all the things His disciples could ask for, they wanted Jesus to teach them how to speak with God. In response, Jesus gave the disciples (and us) a specific pattern for prayer, found in today's Scripture reading and in Jesus's Sermon on the Mount recorded in Matthew 6:9–13. Notice that Jesus kept it simple. Prayer, in its purest form, is a child of God talking to their Father. There doesn't have to be a lot of fanfare or long, passionate displays. Prayer should be easy. Simple. Straightforward.

If you're starting to feel like you're avoiding praying, or find yourself somewhat paralyzed and blank when you begin to pray, remember to start simple. Start with what you're grateful for in life and go from there.

WHERE ARE YOU?

Do you generally feel like you pray out of obligation? Have you looked forward to prayer lately? Explain your answers.

_____

_____

_____

_____

_____

In what ways does your prayer life feel routine?

_____

_____

_____

_____

_____

In what ways has it felt like your prayer life is building your relationship with God?

_____

_____

_____

_____

_____

A PRAYER

Father, please strengthen my prayer time with You by helping me make this time purely about my relationship with You. Help me to see You as a Father. I want to open up and speak with You honestly and take the time to listen to You. In Jesus's name, amen.

DAY 12:
KEEP KNOCKING

SCRIPTURE READING

LUKE 11:5–13 (NIV)

Then Jesus said to them, "Suppose you have a friend, and you go to him at midnight and say, 'Friend, lend me three loaves of bread; a friend of mine on a journey has come to me, and I have no food to offer him.' And suppose the one inside answers, 'Don't bother me. The door is already locked, and my children and I are in bed. I can't get up and give you anything.' I tell you, even though he will not get up and give you the bread because of friendship, yet because of your shameless audacity he will surely get up and give you as much as you need.

"So I say to you: Ask and it will be given to you; seek and you will find; knock and the door will be opened to you. For everyone who asks receives; the one who seeks finds; and to the one who knocks, the door will be opened.

"Which of you fathers, if your son asks for a fish, will give him a snake instead? Or if he asks for an egg, will give him a scorpion? If you then, though you are evil, know how to give good gifts to your children, how much more will your Father in heaven give the Holy Spirit to those who ask him!"

LIFE LESSONS

What do you do when you don't just want something, but you genuinely *need* it? You find a way to get it, don't you? You keep pushing for it, and you don't back down. You know that no one is going to give you what you need. You have to make it happen on your own.

In the culture of Jesus's day, not having food for a visitor would be deeply embarrassing for a host. And that's what makes this story from Jesus so powerful. In the example, the man did whatever it took to get food for his guest, even banging on a neighbor's door and waking up the entire family in the middle of the night! Jesus shared this story because we are to approach God with the same tenacity.

There is so much we will need from God during our lifetime, and He expects us to bring it all to the door—to knock until He opens. We don't need to worry about showing up too often, talking too much, being irritating or bothersome, or asking for something too small or too large. We just need to show up and keep asking. God will respond to our persistence.

WHERE ARE YOU?

What have you found yourself asking God for lately?

_____
_____
_____
_____
_____

Do you believe you are persistent in prayer, or do you think your prayer life could use some work?

_____
_____
_____
_____
_____

What would you like your prayer life to look like?

_____
_____
_____
_____
_____

A PRAYER

Thank You, Father, for responding to us so graciously with patience and love. You are the greatest giver of all, and I know You want to hear from me. Give me the strength and the urgency to be persistent in my prayer life. In Jesus's name, amen.

DAY 13:
UNITED OR UNDONE

SCRIPTURE READING

LUKE 11:14–23 (NIV)

Jesus was driving out a demon that was mute. When the demon left, the man who had been mute spoke, and the crowd was amazed. But some of them said, "By Beelzebul, the prince of demons, he is driving out demons." Others tested him by asking for a sign from heaven.

Jesus knew their thoughts and said to them: "Any kingdom divided against itself will be ruined, and a house divided against itself will fall. If Satan is divided against himself, how can his kingdom stand? I say this because you claim that I drive out demons by Beelzebul. Now if I drive out demons by Beelzebul, by whom do your followers drive them out? So then, they will be your judges. But if I drive out demons by the finger of God, then the kingdom of God has come upon you.

"When a strong man, fully armed, guards his own house, his possessions are safe. But when someone stronger attacks and overpowers him, he takes away the armor in which the man trusted and divides up his plunder.

"Whoever is not with me is against me, and whoever does not gather with me scatters."

LIFE LESSONS

Scripture is full of admonitions about unity among believers. In 1 Corinthians 1:10, Paul says, *"I appeal to you, dear brothers and sisters, by the authority of our Lord Jesus Christ, to live in harmony with each other. Let there be no divisions in the church. Rather, be of one mind, united in thought and purpose"* (NLT). And it's true: fighting within a household is a quick recipe for disaster. Undermining one another and undoing someone else's hard work creates mistrust and anger, sometimes even retaliation, leading to a fast downhill fall.

It might seem strange that, when people accused Jesus of driving out demons in the name of Beelzebul, Jesus chose to talk not about His own authority but about the importance of unity. The real danger isn't outside pressure or dissenters but divisiveness within. He knew that *"any kingdom divided against itself will be ruined"* (Luke 11:17). And that goes both ways: Satan's kingdom can't stand if his demons are driving each other out. Neither can God's kingdom flourish if God's people fail to work together to expand it.

Unity is necessary in order for any work to get done, and we need to be there for each other. Not judging one another's efforts or undoing each other's accomplishments for our own gain, but supporting each other. Trusting one another. As a family, we have to work together with our main purpose in mind: spreading the love of God.

WHERE ARE YOU?

How does this teaching apply to your immediate family?

_____
_____
_____
_____
_____

How does it apply to your family of faith?

_____
_____
_____
_____
_____

In what specific ways can we help bring unity to our families?

_____
_____
_____
_____
_____

What actions would bring division?

_____

_____

_____

_____

A PRAYER

Jesus, I pray for my faith community, that it would be strengthened by our common purpose of walking with You and showing You to the world. Help me to contribute to that unity, to be understanding, patient, and kind. Remind me always of our higher purpose and Your will in our lives. In Your name, amen.

DAY 14:
OUT WITH THE OLD, IN WITH THE NEW

SCRIPTURE READING

LUKE 11:24–26 (NIV)

"When an impure spirit comes out of a person, it goes through arid places seeking rest and does not find it. Then it says, 'I will return to the house I left.' When it arrives, it finds the house swept clean and put in order. Then it goes and takes seven other spirits more wicked than itself, and they go in and live there. And the final condition of that person is worse than the first."

LIFE LESSONS

It's possible to recognize our sin, acknowledge that Jesus paid our debt, and repent—but leave ourselves open to returning to our old selves. Walking with Jesus is a continual endeavor. It takes daily commitment. We don't just wash up once and assume we're good to go for the rest of our lives. We would just accumulate the same filth we spent a bunch of time scrubbing off! No, walking with Jesus is about being made new again and again.

Being with Jesus means walking with Him and filling ourselves with more of Him every day. There is no one-and-done in terms of our Christian walk. We don't just get rid of everything bad and assume it'll stay that way. Instead, we have to effectively fill those spaces in our lives that we've cleaned out.

It's not just about repenting, it's about replacing! The old habits, the old ways—these have to be replaced by something else or they'll find they have a clear path back in. We have to fill our lives with new habits and fill our hearts with God's Spirit so there is no room for unwanted houseguests seeking to return.

WHERE ARE YOU?

What does it mean that "the final condition of that person is worse than the first" (Luke 11:26)?

_____

_____

_____

_____

_____

Describe a time when you repented of your sin, only to later find yourself right back at the same place spiritually.

_____

_____

_____

_____

_____

How can we fill ourselves with more of God's Spirit on a daily basis?

_____

_____

_____

_____

_____

A PRAYER

Jesus, I know that following You is a journey, not a one-time event. Remind me to look for You every day and to create new habits that bring me closer to You so You can fill me with things of Your Spirit. Help me to be so filled with You that there isn't space for old habits and old ways that are not of You. In Your name, amen.

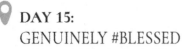

DAY 15:
GENUINELY #BLESSED

SCRIPTURE READING

LUKE 11:27–28 (NIV)

As Jesus was saying these things, a woman in the crowd called out, "Blessed is the mother who gave you birth and nursed you."

He replied, "Blessed rather are those who hear the word of God and obey it."

LIFE LESSONS

The word *blessed* is thrown about rather liberally today. We find it popping up across social media in the hashtag #blessed, people bring it up constantly in prayers, and it's sprinkled into conversation to refer to anything that's gone remotely well in someone's life. But what does it really mean in the Bible to be blessed?

Blessed denotes a connection with God, a link that leads to an inner well-being you can't get anywhere else. God's favors don't just help us externally. Those who are blessed by God have a genuine joy and internal contentment that only that connection with Him can bring.

When the woman blessed Jesus's mother for being so favored as to give birth to our Savior, Jesus reminded the crowd of what really blesses our lives: hearing God's word and obeying it. That is how you will find inner peace and satisfaction.

The most fulfilled life you can imagine, the most blessed, will come from seeking God and living out His will by listening to Him and obeying.

WHERE ARE YOU?

What major blessings has God brought to your life so far?

_____

_____

_____

_____

Are you missing out on blessings because you are hearing God's Word but not applying it?

_____

_____

_____

_____

_____

How can we become better "doers" of God's will?

_____

_____

_____

_____

_____

A PRAYER

Jesus, I want Your blessings in my life. I want this connection with You that comes from listening to You and obeying Your will. I know it is the only way to find true satisfaction in this world. Help me to find fulfillment in You. In Your name, amen.

DAY 16:
ONE ULTIMATE SIGN

SCRIPTURE READING

LUKE 11:29–32 (NIV)

As the crowds increased, Jesus said, "This is a wicked generation. It asks for a sign, but none will be given it except the sign of Jonah. For as Jonah was a sign to the Ninevites, so also will the Son of Man be to this generation. The Queen of the South will rise at the judgment with the people of this generation and condemn them, for she came from the ends of the earth to listen to Solomon's wisdom; and now something greater than Solomon is here. The men of Nineveh will stand up at the judgment with this generation and condemn it, for they repented at the preaching of Jonah; and now something greater than Jonah is here."

LIFE LESSONS

We tend to make everything about us: we want our own explanations, our own proofs, our own "insider moments." This was true back in Bible times, too. Many people around Jesus kept wanting additional proof that He was who He said He was. They kept wanting more. They'd seen signs, they'd heard the teachings, yet they still refused to be satisfied.

Jesus assured the people that He would give them all one sign, but that for some, it still wouldn't be enough. Some people would never see, their eyes would never open, no matter how prevalent God was around them. Jesus's ultimate sign—His reference to Jonah's three days in the belly of a great fish—was His death, burial, and resurrection over the course of three days.

Jesus's taking on our debts and sacrificing Himself for us should be the clincher. It should be all anyone needs to believe. We shouldn't need ideal circumstances, more comfortable lives, answers to all our questions, or a personal-sized miracle signed "with love, from God" to know that He loves us and that He is who He said He is. He already gave us a sign. He already showed us His incredible love.

If your belief in God wavers with what's going on around you, it's possible that you're not really accepting that one ultimate sign: Jesus sacrificed Himself for you and me. Love doesn't get more incredible than that.

WHERE ARE YOU?

Do you find your faith wavering depending on your circumstances?

_____

_____

_____

_____

Do you know anyone who is waiting on their own personal sign from God?

_____

_____

_____

_____

Why is it "wicked" that the people kept asking for a sign?

_____

_____

_____

_____

A PRAYER

Jesus, we need You, our Savior, more than any other sign out there. What You've done for us is incredible. Help us to never forget, under any circumstances, how much You've taken on in our place. I pray that we wouldn't sit around waiting for more signs when we should be focused on following and listening to You. In Your name, amen.

DAY 17:
A LIFE THAT SHINES

SCRIPTURE READING

LUKE 11:33 (NLT)

"No one lights a lamp and then hides it or puts it under a basket. Instead, a lamp is placed on a stand, where its light can be seen by all who enter the house."

LIFE LESSONS

Light from a lamp doesn't just shine—it brightens a room, illuminating the dark corners, preventing us from hurting ourselves, and giving us perspective for our surroundings. Yet in order to illuminate an area, light has to be brought into that space and shined into the darkness. A light that doesn't shine can't fulfill its purpose. And a light that is covered can only illuminate the people closest to it.

The hope, the wonderful message we have, isn't meant to be sequestered away, only available to the few already in the know. Extending beyond your comfort zone, getting out into the world so others can see your light, is vital. Yet it requires you to leave your bubble and make new friends, do new things that pull you out of your routine, and be open and loving even when it's hard.

If we are not out in the world, shining our light, who will bring light to those still living in darkness, to people who've lost their way, who can't find the way out? Who will bring them hope? Your life is the example. Your words, your heart, your love for others is all part of God's light. How you shine is important.

Note: In the next few days, you will find some of Jesus's teachings repeated. Christ already taught these principles to His disciples, and in these passages, He is teaching them to the Pharisees. We will study them again not only because they are important parts of the Bible, but because repetition helps us to learn as we grow in our walk with Jesus. It allows us to dig deeper into the truths of His Word.

WHERE ARE YOU?

In what ways can the characteristics of light and its function be compared to Christians and their role in the world?

_____
_____
_____
_____
_____

How can others see God's light shining through your life?

_____
_____
_____
_____
_____

What could you do to make your light be visible to more people?

_____
_____
_____
_____
_____

A PRAYER

Jesus, You are the Light of the World. Help me to shine in a way that honors You and represents You. Help me to bring light to dark places, hope to hurt people, and love to those who are different from me. In Your name, amen.

DAY 18:
LET THE LIGHT IN

SCRIPTURE READING

LUKE 11:34–36 (NIV)

"Your eye is the lamp of your body. When your eyes are healthy, your whole body also is full of light. But when they are unhealthy, your body also is full of darkness. See to it, then, that the light within you is not darkness. Therefore, if your whole body is full of light, and no part of it dark, it will be just as full of light as when a lamp shines its light on you."

LIFE LESSONS

It's easy to get caught up in trivial, everyday issues: arguing over small things, wanting to be right, critiquing the people around us, clinging to the religious processes and routines we grew up with, remaining in a bubble of comfort and safety. Sound familiar? There are so many things happening around us all the time that are not a big deal in terms of eternity. When we focus on them, we end up looking through a lens of our own making—one that causes us to fail to see the big picture and to appropriately perceive what is going on around us and what God wants for us.

Choosing to view the world through that skewed lens—focusing on those things—causes us to be partially blind, spiritually speaking. We end up with dark corners, blind spots, and miss out on what God wants us to see. We fail to let in all of the light by closing ourselves off, by only looking inward or viewing the world with closed and distracted hearts and minds instead of open ones.

What does it mean to truly see, to actually let the light in? And *how* do you do that? It starts by living life with your eyes open, ready to receive what's happening around you with an open heart. This means focusing on things that matter to God: things that are important and eternal.

WHERE ARE YOU?

In your own words, how are our spiritual eyes the lamp for our bodies?

_____

_____

_____

_____

_____

How healthy do you think your eyes are?

_____

_____

_____

_____

_____

How might you be creating dark corners where the light isn't reaching?

_____

_____

_____

_____

_____

A PRAYER

Jesus, I pray for healthy eyes: eyes that perceive eternal truths, eyes that focus on what's important to You, eyes that aren't distracted by petty issues or judging those around me. I pray that my eyes would let in every bit of Your light so Your light can also shine out of me. In Your name, amen.

DAY 19:
PAGEANTS OF PIETY VERSUS PRACTICES OF HEART

SCRIPTURE READING

LUKE 11:37–54 (MSG)

When he finished that talk, a Pharisee asked him to dinner. He entered his house and sat right down at the table. The Pharisee was shocked and somewhat offended when he saw that Jesus didn't wash up before the meal. But the Master said to him, "I know you Pharisees buff the surface of your cups and plates so they sparkle in the sun, but I also know your insides are maggoty with greed and secret evil. Stupid Pharisees! Didn't the One who made the outside also make the inside? Turn both your pockets and your hearts inside out and give generously to the poor; then your lives will be clean, not just your dishes and your hands.

"I've had it with you! You're hopeless, you Pharisees! Frauds! You keep meticulous account books, tithing on every nickel and dime you get, but manage to find loopholes for getting around basic matters of justice and God's love. Careful bookkeeping is commendable, but the basics are required.

"You're hopeless, you Pharisees! Frauds! You love sitting at the head table at church dinners, love preening yourselves in the radiance of public flattery. Frauds! You're just like unmarked graves: People walk over that nice, grassy surface, never suspecting the rot and corruption that is six feet under."

One of the religion scholars spoke up: "Teacher, do you realize that in saying these things you're insulting us?"

He said, "Yes, and I can be even more explicit. You're hopeless, you religion scholars! You load people down with rules and regulations, nearly breaking their backs, but never lift even a finger to help.

"You're hopeless! You build tombs for the prophets your ancestors killed. The tombs you build are monuments to your murdering ancestors more than to the murdered prophets. That accounts for God's Wisdom saying, 'I will send them prophets and apostles, but they'll kill them and run them off.' What it means is that every drop of righteous blood ever spilled from the time earth began until now, from the blood of Abel to the blood of Zechariah, who was struck down between altar and sanctuary, is on your heads. Yes, it's on the bill of this generation and this generation will pay.

"You're hopeless, you religion scholars! You took the key of knowledge, but instead of unlocking doors, you locked them. You won't go in yourself, and won't let anyone else in either."

As soon as Jesus left the table, the religion scholars and Pharisees went into a rage. They went over and over everything he said, plotting how they could trap him in something from his own mouth.

LIFE LESSONS

You might have heard this saying before: sitting in a carport doesn't make you a pickup truck. Likewise, going to church doesn't make you a Christian. If we're not careful, we can mistake our outward actions for inward purity, which, in turn, leads us down a road that might not even include a relationship with God.

The Pharisees were professionals at outward modification. They had perfected the rules and regulations. They could exhibit their "higher morality" without truly speaking to God or doing anything out of love for someone else. But if you just watched their external actions, you would assume they lived a moral life. These men limited themselves to certain highly visible practices of piety while steamrolling over others for their own benefit and superiority.

God doesn't desire a pageant of who can follow rules the best or put on the best display. God desires a purity that leads to practice. He wants us to have a servant's heart; He wants us to give, not take. He wants committed effort that starts within the heart itself.

WHERE ARE YOU?

Have most of your actions lately been externally or internally motivated? Can you give a couple of life examples of each?

_____

_____

_____

_____

_____

Have you known anyone who outwardly seemed pious but tended to be cruel and selfish on the inside? How did they make you feel?

_____

_____

_____

_____

_____

What do you think Jesus meant when He said the scholars "took the key of knowledge" (Luke 11:52)?

_____

_____

_____

_____

_____

A PRAYER

Jesus, please shine Your light on my heart and my motivations. Reveal to me how spiritually healthy my heart is in Your eyes so I can seek You better. Show me how to love those around me with a servant's heart. Don't let me fall prey to focusing on my external actions and ignore my relationship with You. In Your name, amen.

DAY 20:
A RELATIONSHIP, NOT A ROUTINE

SCRIPTURE READING

LUKE 12:1–3 (NIV)

Meanwhile, when a crowd of many thousands had gathered, so that they were trampling on one another, Jesus began to speak first to his disciples, saying: "Be on your guard against the yeast of the Pharisees, which is hypocrisy. There is nothing concealed that will not be disclosed, or hidden that will not be made known. What you have said in the dark will be heard in the daylight, and what you have whispered in the ear in the inner rooms will be proclaimed from the roofs."

LIFE LESSONS

Many people try to skip the relationship aspect of a walk with Christ—the change of heart. It can be so much easier to follow routines, to simply act accordingly and seem nice and proper. When we play it safe like that, we don't need to do as much internal work. It may seem like we're getting away with it, but we're not. When we skip the heart stuff, we're only hurting ourselves.

Just as yeast spreads through dough, hypocrisy contaminates our walk with Jesus. And it grows. When we start replacing a genuine relationship with external actions, and when we're motivated by how others see us instead of how God sees us, we head down a path that isn't easy to break away from. We quickly turn from a relationship with God to an outward appearance of righteousness.

Lack of a true connection with God, an unchanged heart, leads down the road the Pharisees took. And that hypocrisy may seem hidden, as though no one around us can tell; but, at some point, it'll emerge. Secrets come out. When your life isn't being altered by Christ, it's being altered by something else. And, eventually, everything will be brought into the light when we stand before God.

WHERE ARE YOU?

How is hypocrisy like yeast?

_____

_____

_____

_____

_____

Are you trying to keep any secrets from God? What needs to happen to free you from those things you're trying to hide?

_____

_____

_____

_____

_____

A PRAYER

Jesus, please help me to be authentic in my walk with You. Please reveal any hypocrisy in my heart and help me to turn back to You. In Your name, amen.

DAY 21:
FOCUS ON THE "MORE"

SCRIPTURE READING

LUKE 12:4–7 (NIV)

"I tell you, my friends, do not be afraid of those who kill the body and after that can do no more. But I will show you whom you should fear: Fear him who, after your body has been killed, has authority to throw you into hell. Yes, I tell you, fear him. Are not five sparrows sold for two pennies? Yet not one of them is forgotten by God. Indeed, the very hairs of your head are all numbered. Don't be afraid; you are worth more than many sparrows."

LIFE LESSONS

Most people put death at the top of the list of things they fear the most. Completely understandable. The process of dying is scary and hard to imagine, let alone become okay with. But for us believers, death is not the end. Our lives are ultimately held in God's hands. He gives us the opportunity to step into His presence. Far more worrisome than death is the thought of an afterlife *without* God.

Jesus knew He would be beaten, humiliated, despised, rejected, and then crucified. Yet He didn't fear man or death. He knew He was following His Father's plan. He knew there were worse things than physical pain and earthly cruelty, that there was a lot more to lose.

Life on earth can be hard, but there is more coming. And that *more* is where we need to keep our eyes glued.

WHERE ARE YOU?

Rewrite Luke 12:4 in your own words, focusing on how it relates to your own life and the fears that overwhelm your fear of God.

_____

_____

_____

_____

_____

How does knowing how much God values you impact how you approach fear?

_____

_____

_____

_____

_____

How can a healthy fear of God lead you to follow Him with a fearless attitude toward the world?

_____

_____

_____

_____

_____

A PRAYER

Jesus, help me to live for You alone. I pray that I would develop a reverent fear of You. May my worship of You spiritually give me the boldness to live without fear of what can happen to me physically. In Your name, amen.

DAY 22:
CONSTANT VISIBILITY

SCRIPTURE READING

LUKE 12:8–9 (NIV)

I tell you, whoever publicly acknowledges me before others, the Son of Man will also acknowledge before the angels of God. But whoever disowns me before others will be disowned before the angels of God.

LIFE LESSONS

Our lives and our actions are constantly visible to others—especially now, in our social-media culture, where we are potentially being watched and evaluated by strangers and friends alike every time we walk out the door, go to a restaurant, or post on social media. Being constantly visible means that we need to constantly consider what our actions and our words say about us. Do our actions show God's love? Do our words spread hope and compassion? Do we acknowledge God in the things we do and say?

Acknowledging God is about far more than just declaring you're a Christian. It's a lifestyle. It's about being a representation of His character. When our actions, our words, how we treat other people, and how we love others don't reflect Jesus—when they have nothing to do with Him and His message—we are refusing to acknowledge Him.

Your life should reveal Christ's character in everything you say or do—whether in person or online.

WHERE ARE YOU?

What does it mean for your life to acknowledge God publicly?

_____

_____

_____

_____

_____

Considering your answer above, does your life confess Jesus or deny Him?

_____

_____

_____

_____

_____

How can you acknowledge Christ openly through your words and actions?

_____

_____

_____

_____

_____

A PRAYER

Jesus, I want my words and actions to reflect You and my walk with You. I pray that my lifestyle would support my words. I pray for a heart and a character that continually grows more like You as I seek You. Please help me to live today in light of eternity. In Your name, amen.

DAY 23:
FINDING THE WORDS

SCRIPTURE READING

LUKE 12:10–12 (NIV)

"And everyone who speaks a word against the Son of Man will be forgiven, but anyone who blasphemes against the Holy Spirit will not be forgiven.

"When you are brought before synagogues, rulers and authorities, do not worry about how you will defend yourselves or what you will say, for the Holy Spirit will teach you at that time what you should say."

LIFE LESSONS

Have you ever been afraid to speak about God? Have you hesitated to respond to someone's questions about God because you felt you didn't have the knowledge or the understanding to respond appropriately? It's easy to freeze up, not wanting to risk being wrong or saying something that makes us look foolish or ignorant.

But you don't have to have the right words! Jesus is a flawless Teacher. If your heart is following His, then the Holy Spirit will speak through you. *"The Holy Spirit will teach you at that time what you should say"* (verse 12). Jesus said in John 16:13 that the Spirit will guide us into all truth.

So, when you're feeling in over your head, say a little prayer, focus on God, know that He's standing with You, and speak with love.

WHERE ARE YOU?

How do you think the Holy Spirit teaches us what to say?

_____

_____

_____

_____

_____

How are you trusting in the Holy Spirit to guide you on a daily basis?

_____

_____

_____

_____

_____

In what ways can we become more open to the Holy Spirit and listen to the Spirit so He can speak through us?

_____

_____

_____

_____

_____

A PRAYER

Holy Spirit, fill my heart with Your teaching and help my mouth to speak Your truth. Thank You for always being with me, working in me and empowering my life. In Jesus's name, amen.

DAY 24:
LIFE'S GREATEST TREASURE

SCRIPTURE READING

LUKE 12:13–21 (MSG)

Someone out of the crowd said, "Teacher, order my brother to give me a fair share of the family inheritance."

He replied, "Mister, what makes you think it's any of my business to be a judge or mediator for you?"

Speaking to the people, he went on, "Take care! Protect yourself against the least bit of greed. Life is not defined by what you have, even when you have a lot."

Then he told them this story: "The farm of a certain rich man produced a terrific crop. He talked to himself: 'What can I do? My barn isn't big enough for this harvest.' Then he said, 'Here's what I'll do: I'll tear down my barns and build bigger ones. Then I'll gather in all my grain and goods, and I'll say to myself, Self, you've done well! You've got it made and can now retire. Take it easy and have the time of your life!'

"Just then God showed up and said, 'Fool! Tonight you die. And your barnful of goods—who gets it?'

"That's what happens when you fill your barn with Self and not with God."

LIFE LESSONS

The most valuable thing in life isn't a *thing*, and the greatest treasure is not earthly riches. If you've found yourself running the rat race, exhausting your time and energy to acquire a certain level of lifestyle, it's time to reflect on what really matters.

The richest people in God's eyes are those who have a right relationship with Him. The farmer in Jesus's story *lived* for more crops and bigger barns. He focused entirely on that concept of "more." This man thought that if he could store up enough earthly wealth, then his life would be complete. But, in the end, he would lose it all regardless.

It is foolish to seek after temporary things that won't last while failing to pursue a relationship with Jesus that will last forever. The greatest treasure is one the world cannot take away: a personal relationship with Jesus.

WHERE ARE YOU?

Do you feel that you've been focused more on earthly riches or on an eternal relationship with Jesus? In what ways specifically?

_____
_____
_____
_____
_____

What would change in your spiritual life if you sought after Jesus as the greatest treasure?

_____
_____
_____
_____
_____

What would change in how you live each day?

_____
_____
_____
_____
_____

A PRAYER

Jesus, I don't want to waste my life seeking more money or more things that won't last. Please, give me Your perspective when it comes to how to spend my time. Help me to stop and reconsider when I get off track, when I get distracted by the world around me. Nothing compares to my relationship with You. Help me to seek after You as life's greatest treasure. In Your name, amen.

DAY 25:
WHAT REALLY MATTERS

SCRIPTURE READING

LUKE 12:22–34 (MSG)

He continued this subject with his disciples. "Don't fuss about what's on the table at mealtimes or if the clothes in your closet are in fashion. There is far more to your inner life than the food you put in your stomach, more to your outer appearance than the clothes you hang on your body. Look at the ravens, free and unfettered, not tied down to a job description, carefree in the care of God. And you count far more.

"Has anyone by fussing before the mirror ever gotten taller by so much as an inch? If fussing can't even do that, why fuss at all? Walk into the fields and look at the wildflowers. They don't fuss with their appearance—but have you ever seen color and design quite like it? The ten best-dressed men and women in the country look shabby alongside them. If God gives such attention to the wildflowers, most of them never even seen, don't you think he'll attend to you, take pride in you, do his best for you?

"What I'm trying to do here is get you to relax, not be so preoccupied with getting so you can respond to God's giving. People who don't know God and the way he works fuss over these things, but you know both God and how he works. Steep yourself in God-reality, God-initiative, God-provisions. You'll find all your everyday human concerns will be met. Don't be afraid of missing out. You're my dearest friends! The Father wants to give you the very kingdom itself.

"Be generous. Give to the poor. Get yourselves a bank that can't go bankrupt, a bank in heaven far from bank robbers, safe from embezzlers, a bank you can bank on. It's obvious, isn't it? The place where your treasure is, is the place you will most want to be, and end up being."

LIFE LESSONS

If you find yourself stressing most days about whether your job is good enough, whether your clothes look okay, or any number of things related to you how society perceives you, you are not alone. Even people in biblical times had these concerns. But constantly worrying about wealth doesn't guide us toward happiness and contentment. It leads to a life of anxiety, which is not what God wants for us.

The good news is that we can change our definition of what really matters and find a more peaceful and productive life. Rather than worrying about things outside of our control, we should be trusting in the One who controls all things. He promises to take care of us.

This life will not last forever. Our home with Jesus is our future, and *that* should be our focus.

WHERE ARE YOU?

What is your definition of "worry"?

_____

_____

_____

_____

What are you currently worried about?

_____

_____

_____

_____

According to this Scripture passage, how can you have peace that your future reward is safe and secure?

_____

_____

_____

_____

A PRAYER

God, give me the mind of Christ so that I can have the right perspective on money and being part of this world. I don't want a selfish life of anxiety but a contented life trusting in You. Help me to focus on You and treasures that last forever. In Jesus's name, amen.

DAY 26:
PREPPED AND READY

SCRIPTURE READING

LUKE 12:35–40 (MSG)

"Keep your shirts on; keep the lights on! Be like house servants waiting for their master to come back from his honeymoon, awake and ready to open the door when he arrives and knocks. Lucky the servants whom the master finds on watch! He'll put on an apron, sit them at the table, and serve them a meal, sharing his wedding feast with them. It doesn't matter what time of the night he arrives; they're awake—and so blessed!

"You know that if the house owner had known what night the burglar was coming, he wouldn't have stayed out late and left the place unlocked. So don't you be lazy and careless. Just when you don't expect him, the Son of Man will show up."

LIFE LESSONS

If you knew when a thief was on the way to your house, you would prepare yourself by locking the doors and calling the police. If you knew exactly when a tornado would hit your town, you would gather some belongings and hightail it out of there, spreading the word as you left. If God told you the very second you would be meeting Jesus, you would immediately go about getting your life in order, prepped and ready spiritually for His appearance.

We can't know any of those things. Only God does. But we do know that we will come face-to-face with Jesus *someday*. Since we don't know when, we should be living every day in preparation for Him. We should be making each day count by actively loving like Jesus: being kind to the people around us, building others up in our relationships, creating art, enjoying nature's beauty, and putting in our own best efforts to help reshape society so we can offer support to those in need, protect the vulnerable, and extend a welcoming hand to anyone who is struggling.

WHERE ARE YOU?

How does the element of surprise lead to proper preparation?

_____

_____

_____

_____

_____

How are you living each day ready for Jesus's return?

_____

_____

_____

_____

_____

What needs to change in your life so that you will be ready to meet Jesus, regardless of when that happens?

_____

_____

_____

_____

_____

A PRAYER

Jesus, I pray that I'll be ready to meet You when the time comes. Help me to keep my eyes on You and the knowledge of eternity in my heart, so I can live every day in such a way that I will be ready no matter what, making each day count. In Your name, amen.

SCRIPTURE READING

LUKE 12:41–48 (NIV)

Peter asked, "Lord, are you telling this parable to us, or to everyone?"

The Lord answered, "Who then is the faithful and wise manager, whom the master puts in charge of his servants to give them their food allowance at the proper time? It will be good for that servant whom the master finds doing so when he returns. Truly I tell you, he will put him in charge of all his possessions. But suppose the servant says to himself, 'My master is taking a long time in coming,' and he then begins to beat the other servants, both men and women, and to eat and drink and get drunk. The master of that servant will come on a day when he does not expect him and at an hour he is not aware of. He will cut him to pieces and assign him a place with the unbelievers.

"The servant who knows the master's will and does not get ready or does not do what the master wants will be beaten with many blows. But the one who does not know and does things deserving punishment will be beaten with few blows. From everyone who has been given much, much will be demanded; and from the one who has been entrusted with much, much more will be asked."

LIFE LESSONS

God has left the world and the people in it in our temporary care. We are His messengers and His hands. We're supposed to be taking care of each other, supporting one another, loving those around us, and actively pursuing God.

In this parable, we are the servants and Jesus represents the master. When a master gives his servant responsibilities, he will always find out whether the servant fulfilled his duties. The time of reckoning happens when the master returns to see how well his servants have carried out his instructions.

Jesus has opened our eyes and given us responsibilities as we've walked with Him. Upon His return, what will He find?

WHERE ARE YOU?

How are you doing with the responsibilities that God has entrusted to you?

_____

_____

_____

_____

_____

"From everyone who has been given much, much will be demanded; and from the one who has been entrusted with much, much more will be asked" *(Luke 12:48 NIV). What do you think of this verse? How might it be applicable to your own responsibilities?*

_____

_____

_____

_____

_____

A PRAYER

Jesus, You opened my eyes and let me walk with You. Help me to serve You as You've asked; help me to fulfill the purpose You've given me. You have always been faithful to me. Help me to be faithful to You in return. In Your name, amen.

DAY 28:
STICKING WITH THE SOLD-OUTS

SCRIPTURE READING

LUKE 12:49–53 (NLT)

"I have come to set the world on fire, and I wish it were already burning! I have a terrible baptism of suffering ahead of me, and I am under a heavy burden until it is accomplished. Do you think I have come to bring peace to the earth? No, I have come to divide people against each other! From now on families will be split apart, three in favor of me, and two against—or two in favor and three against.

> *'Father will be divided against son*
> *and son against father;*
> *mother against daughter*
> *and daughter against mother;*
> *and mother-in-law against daughter-in-law*
> *and daughter-in-law against mother-in-law.'"*

LIFE LESSONS

True discipleship divides the sold-outs, who are all in, from the sell-outs, who do whatever is better for them in the moment. Many people who call themselves "Christians" only follow God when it is convenient; they're Christians as long as they don't have to give up or change anything. Others are simply complacent; they don't want to do the work. When following Jesus gets uncomfortable, they abandon their faith and do their own thing.

On your journey with Christ, you will walk alongside people who fall away, their hearts growing cold to God. Do not let them sway you. As hard as it can be, following Christ wholeheartedly can mean leaving people behind. Stick with Him! Your eternal, spiritual relationship with God as your Father is more important than any temporary physical relationship on earth.

WHERE ARE YOU?

What do you think Jesus meant by the statement "I have come to set the world on fire" (Luke 12:49)?

_____

_____

_____

_____

_____

In what ways have you grown complacent in your journey with Jesus?

_____

_____

_____

_____

_____

What has it cost you to follow Him?

_____

_____

_____

_____

_____

A PRAYER

Jesus, there are times in my life when I have grown complacent in my journey with You. Please forgive me for the times I've walked away from You toward whatever was easier for me. Increase my determination and expand my vision of the things of eternity, so that I will always keep making my way toward You. In Your name, amen.

DAY 29:
SEEKING LEADS TO SIGNS

SCRIPTURE READING

LUKE 12:54–56 (NLT)

Then Jesus turned to the crowd and said, "When you see clouds beginning to form in the west, you say, 'Here comes a shower.' And you are right. When the south wind blows, you say, 'Today will be a scorcher.' And it is. You fools! You know how to interpret the weather signs of the earth and sky, but you don't know how to interpret the present times."

LIFE LESSONS

We make room for so many small, insignificant things in the world around us: we learn how to predict seasons and climates, how to manage social media, where to go for the best Italian food, which route is the fastest way to our favorite grocery store at certain times of day. Yet how often do we fail to spend time looking for God and trying to understand Him?

The signs of God's presence are everywhere, but how easily we miss them! God desires to reveal Himself to those who truly seek Him. The problem is that we tend to chase after earthly pursuits more than we pursue Him. When we seek God more, we gain more insight into His will, the signs of His presence, and His desires for the world and our lives. Prioritizing Him will always be worth it.

WHERE ARE YOU?

In what ways do you seek earthly knowledge over godly wisdom?

_____

_____

_____

_____

_____

List some signs of God's presence in your life.

A PRAYER

Jesus, please help me to keep my eyes on You. I know You are always there, surrounding us. Help me to watch for You daily and walk with You diligently. I want to desire to know You over any earthly knowledge. In Your name, amen.

DAY 30:
SETTLE YOUR OWN ACCOUNTS

SCRIPTURE READING
....

LUKE 12:57–59 (NLT)

"Why can't you decide for yourselves what is right? When you are on the way to court with your accuser, try to settle the matter before you get there. Otherwise, your accuser may drag you before the judge, who will hand you over to an officer, who will throw you into prison. And if that happens, you won't be free again until you have paid the very last penny."

LIFE LESSONS
....

The lengthy discussion recorded in Luke's gospel that we have been reviewing for the past several days all began when a man confronted Jesus about his brother's greed. In Luke 12:13, this man said to Jesus, *"Teacher, order my brother to give me a fair share of the family inheritance"* (MSG). Jesus then spent the next forty-four verses turning the situation into a spiritual lesson warning about worldly possessions, His own return, and the upcoming divisions that would take place in His name.

Now, in Luke 12:57–59, Jesus returns to the man's original request. He clarifies that we need to have our own matters resolved, our accounts for our lives settled, before His return. We have to choose for ourselves how we will lead our lives, what we will focus on, and who we will live for. He can't decide for us.

This means choosing how we want to lead our lives today—not ten or twenty years from now. We can't put everything off until the end. We can't wait for the last moment to turn things around or slip in some good deeds. There won't be a special moment when Jesus comes down to tell us that it's time to start living differently before we regret it. That time is now.

WHERE ARE YOU?

What do you think it means when Jesus says to settle the matter before you get to court?

_____

_____

_____

_____

_____

When has Jesus taken your earthly requests and turned them into spiritual lessons?

_____

_____

_____

_____

_____

A PRAYER

Jesus, I pray that I would choose well every single day. I also pray for others, those who haven't accepted You yet, that they would come to know You and settle their accounts before it's too late. Help me to be an example with my own life so others will seek after You. In Your name, amen.

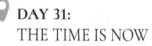

DAY 31:
THE TIME IS NOW

SCRIPTURE READING

LUKE 13:1–5 (CEV)

About this same time Jesus was told that Pilate had given orders for some people from Galilee to be killed while they were offering sacrifices. Jesus replied:

> *Do you think that these people were worse sinners than everyone else in Galilee just because of what happened to them? Not at all! But you can be sure that if you don't turn back to God, every one of you will also be killed. What about those eighteen people who died when the tower in Siloam fell on them? Do you think they were worse than everyone else in Jerusalem? Not at all! But you can be sure that if you don't turn back to God, every one of you will also die.*

LIFE LESSONS

We don't know the future. We don't know when tragedy will strike or our time on this earth will come to an end. Our lives are delicate, our bodies fragile.

Here, Jesus compares people who were slaughtered in the temple while worshipping God to those who perished in what sounds like a freak accident. What do both have in common? None of them knew it was coming. None of them had any control over those circumstances. What *did* they have control over? The decisions they made while they were alive.

We may push God back, thinking, "Tomorrow I'll have time to really dedicate myself to this," but Jesus wants us to see the suddenness with which we might lose that opportunity. If you've been struggling to step into action, it's important to remember that it *is* possible to delay too long. As easy as it is to slide into our own comfortable routines, we have to remember how unpredictable life is and how precious and fleeting our days on earth are.

WHERE ARE YOU?

Why do you think Jesus kept emphasizing that these people who died were no worse, no more sinful, than anyone else?

_____

_____

_____

_____

_____

What things in your life have reminded you of life's fragility?

_____

_____

_____

_____

_____

What aspects of your life might you be putting off that need to be taken care of sooner rather than later?

_____

_____

_____

_____

_____

_____

A PRAYER

God, I recognize how fragile and unpredictable our lives are. Thank You for preparing a place in heaven with You where there is no suffering, no crying, and no pain. I pray for all of us who have yet to choose a heart of action **and** movement, that we would be reminded not to delay and to seize the opportunity before it's too late. In Your name, amen.

DAY 32:
SEASONS OF MERCY

SCRIPTURE READING

. . . .

LUKE 13:6–9 (CEV)

Jesus then told them this story:

> *A man had a fig tree growing in his vineyard. One day he went out to pick some figs, but he didn't find any. So he said to the gardener, "For three years I have come looking for figs on this tree, and I haven't found any yet. Chop it down! Why should it take up space?"*
>
> *The gardener answered, "Master, leave it for another year. I'll dig around it and put some manure on it to make it grow. Maybe it will have figs on it next year. If it doesn't, you can have it cut down."*

LIFE LESSONS

. . . .

Jesus may warn us that we need to settle our accounts, to commit to Him completely, but He doesn't do that and then leave us to find our way on our own. He is right there with us, coaxing us along, being patient when we take a step back, rejoicing when we take a step forward.

Similar to yesterday's reading, this passage refers to the sensation of having all the time in the world—the mistaken certainty that things can wait until tomorrow. Known as "The Parable of the Barren Fig Tree," it speaks of urgency but also of God's mercy and patience.

Jesus is the patient caretaker who gives us everything we need to be successful in our walk with God, to grow and bear fruit. While our God is gracious, He is *looking* for fruit! He expects fruit! When He does not see fruit, He will mercifully give more of Himself to encourage us toward bearing fruit and doing what we were created to do. But God is not going to wait forever. At some point, the season will end.

Yet even if we've fallen away, if we're reading this, there is still hope and opportunity. He has given us additional time. We can be encouraged to know that God is pulling us back in, giving us what we need, and rooting for us to take steps in the right direction.

WHERE ARE YOU?

In what specific areas of your life do you recognize God's patience?

_____
_____
_____
_____
_____

What resources does God provide us with so we can bear fruit?

_____
_____
_____
_____
_____

In what ways does this passage give you a greater sense of urgency in your relationship with God?

_____
_____
_____
_____
_____

A PRAYER

God, thank You for the patience and perseverance You extend to every single one of us. You give us everything we need. Help us to recognize that and use what You have given us to do Your work. Let our lives be an example to others. In Your name, amen.

DAY 33:
BRINGING BACK COMPASSION

SCRIPTURE READING

LUKE 13:10–17 (NLT)

One Sabbath day as Jesus was teaching in a synagogue, he saw a woman who had been crippled by an evil spirit. She had been bent double for eighteen years and was unable to stand up straight. When Jesus saw her, he called her over and said, "Dear woman, you are healed of your sickness!" Then he touched her, and instantly she could stand straight. How she praised God!

But the leader in charge of the synagogue was indignant that Jesus had healed her on the Sabbath day. "There are six days of the week for working," he said to the crowd. "Come on those days to be healed, not on the Sabbath."

But the Lord replied, "You hypocrites! Each of you works on the Sabbath day! Don't you untie your ox or your donkey from its stall on the Sabbath and lead it out for water? This dear woman, a daughter of Abraham, has been held in bondage by Satan for eighteen years. Isn't it right that she be released, even on the Sabbath?"

This shamed his enemies, but all the people rejoiced at the wonderful things he did.

LIFE LESSONS

We see it every day all around us, on the news, in every corner of the Internet, and within our own circles: a lack of compassion. In fact, many of us are guilty of lacking compassion ourselves. Sure, we may have compassion for animals or children—but when it comes to adults, it's easier for us to judge or criticize them than to offer them help. We make excuses for not stepping up: we're too busy; it's not our responsibility; they made their own choices.

The leaders in today's Scripture passage struggled with compassion too. They would water their donkeys on the Sabbath, a day when no work was to be done. Yet they were upset that Jesus healed people on the same day. To them, taking care of their animals on the Sabbath was acceptable. Taking care of a human? Not so much.

Scripture records seven miracles that Jesus completed on the Sabbath. With these miracles, Jesus charges us to help others even if it goes against tradition and expectations, even if it's inconvenient or against cultural norms. Yes, it's important for us to be safe when helping others, but we need to stop finding excuses to walk away from someone in need. We have to start seeing others with the compassionate eyes of Jesus.

WHERE ARE YOU?

How does the woman's physical impediment relate to other kinds of spiritual bondage in this story?

_____

_____

_____

_____

Do you believe the leaders were indignant just because it was the Sabbath, or did they have other reasons as well? What might those reasons be?

_____

_____

_____

_____

What stops you from having compassion for other people?

_____

_____

_____

_____

A PRAYER

Jesus, thank You for Your healing and for releasing us from our own types of bondage. I pray for a compassionate heart, that I would see what You see when I look at the people around me. I pray that I would always remember the worth of those around me, knowing that You love them just as much as You love me. In Your name, amen.

DAY 34:
EXPONENTIAL IMPACT

SCRIPTURE READING

LUKE 13:18–19 (NLT)

Then Jesus said, "What is the Kingdom of God like? How can I illustrate it? It is like a tiny mustard seed that a man planted in a garden; it grows and becomes a tree, and the birds make nests in its branches."

LIFE LESSONS

Have you ever wondered if your actions make any difference? After all, you're just one person. Well, consider this: what may start with the tiniest bit of faith in one person can grow rapidly. And when it grows, it doesn't just make *that person's* faith bigger; it grows outward, spreading far and wide. It affects the circle of people around the initial person and then the circles of people around *them*.

Jesus used the image of a mustard seed to illustrate this exponential impact. In Matthew 17, Jesus challenged His disciples to have faith like a mustard seed, and here in Luke 13, He compares the kingdom of God to a mustard seed. Mustard seeds are so tiny they are barely visible to the human eye. But they can grow into huge, expansive trees with long, impressive branches. What begins as something tiny becomes large enough to house birds and provide shelter for God's creations.

Never underestimate your influence. God's kingdom grows exponentially in the lives of those who put their faith in Him and decide to be like Christ. You may not be able to see it from where you're standing, but know that your impact is larger than you think!

WHERE ARE YOU?

What size would you guess your faith is currently?

How is it growing in your life right now?

_____

_____

_____

_____

How does the idea of birds making nests in branches coincide with your faith life?

_____

_____

_____

_____

In what ways do you think God can grow your life exponentially?

_____

_____

_____

_____

A PRAYER

God, help me to have faith, even if it's just the size of a mustard seed. Then, help my faith to grow. I pray that my influence on people would be one reflective of Your character and Your heart. Thank You for using me even when I can only give a little. In Your name, amen.

DAY 35:
A GREATER PURPOSE

SCRIPTURE READING

LUKE 13:20–21 (NLT)

He also asked, "What else is the Kingdom of God like? It is like the yeast a woman used in making bread. Even though she put only a little yeast in three measures of flour, it permeated every part of the dough."

LIFE LESSONS

Our lives often feel small and inconsequential, yet be assured that a life of faith is anything but that—even if it can be difficult to see or measure.

Jesus often used the properties of yeast as an illustration in His teachings. When He was speaking of the Pharisees, He frequently referred to yeast to symbolize sin and contamination. Here, however, He compared the kingdom of God to yeast.

Yeast makes dough into something entirely new and better—something with a greater purpose, a renewed purpose. We are surrounded all the time by a broken world and lost people, but if we're walking with Jesus, if He's working through us, we can touch so many lives. God can use our small faith to start permeating the lives of others. And our lives, so small in the grand scheme of things, are given a greater and renewed purpose, able to be much more than they could ever have been with only our own efforts.

WHERE ARE YOU?

Can you think of other ways the yeast in the dough represents God's kingdom or God's work in our lives?

_____

_____

_____

_____

_____

How has God been giving your life a greater purpose? How has this influenced your community or the world?

_____

_____

_____

_____

_____

A PRAYER

God, work through me so that I can influence this world for the better in Your name. Help me to discover my greater purpose and give me the courage to live it. Thank You for giving each of us our own gifts that help us to bring Your light to a dark world. In Jesus's name, amen.

DAY 36:
IN IT FOR THE LONG HAUL

SCRIPTURE READING

JOHN 10:22–38 (NLT)

It was now winter, and Jesus was in Jerusalem at the time of Hanukkah, the Festival of Dedication. He was in the Temple, walking through the section known as Solomon's Colonnade. The people surrounded him and asked, "How long are you going to keep us in suspense? If you are the Messiah, tell us plainly."

Jesus replied, "I have already told you, and you don't believe me. The proof is the work I do in my Father's name. But you don't believe me because you are not my sheep. My sheep listen to my voice; I know them, and they follow me. I give them eternal life, and they will never perish. No one can snatch them away from me, for my Father has given them to me, and he is more powerful than anyone else. No one can snatch them from the Father's hand. The Father and I are one."

Once again the people picked up stones to kill him. Jesus said, "At my Father's direction I have done many good works. For which one are you going to stone me?"

They replied, "We're stoning you not for any good work, but for blasphemy! You, a mere man, claim to be God."

Jesus replied, "It is written in your own Scriptures that God said to certain leaders of the people, 'I say, you are gods!' And you know that the Scriptures cannot be altered. So if those people who received God's message were called 'gods,' why do you call it blasphemy when I say, 'I am the Son of God'? After all, the Father set me apart and sent me into the world. Don't believe me unless I carry out my Father's work. But if I do his work, believe in the evidence of the miraculous works I have done, even if you don't believe me. Then you will know and understand that the Father is in me, and I am in the Father."

LIFE LESSONS

The Festival (or Feast) of Dedication is a Jewish celebration that commemorates the rededication of the temple in Jerusalem. It is also known as Hanukkah. This event goes on for eight days in honor of the miracle that occurred when the temple was originally rededicated by Judas Maccabaeus in 165 BC. According to rabbinic tradition, God caused the eternal flame to burn for eight days on *one day's worth* of oil.

Jesus is more than capable of keeping the fire burning forever; the Holy Spirit is in it with us for the long haul. We can't be taken from Jesus without our consent, and we can never be lost as long as we're listening for His voice. All we have to do is continue to choose Him. As we've read before, He will always be calling to us, giving us the resources to flourish as He burns inside of us and waits beside us.

WHERE ARE YOU?

Do you trust more in your ability to hold on to God or His ability to hold on to you? Explain your answer.

_____

_____

_____

_____

_____

Why is it important that Jesus says, "My Father has given them to me" (John 10:29 NLT) in reference to His followers?

_____

_____

_____

_____

_____

How is the fire of the Holy Spirit burning in your heart?

_____

_____

_____

_____

_____

A PRAYER

God, thank You for holding on to me, for keeping me close and calling to me when I stray. Thank You for the miracle of salvation. Help me to find peace and rest in Your arms, knowing You will never stop calling me. In Jesus's name, amen.

DAY 37:
PERFECTLY TIMED

SCRIPTURE READING

JOHN 10:39–42 (NIV)

Again they tried to seize him, but he escaped their grasp.

Then Jesus went back across the Jordan to the place where John had been baptizing in the early days. There he stayed, and many people came to him. They said, "Though John never performed a sign, all that John said about this man was true." And in that place many believed in Jesus.

LIFE LESSONS

On more than one occasion, people wanted to stone Jesus, to kill Him, because they couldn't accept His claim of being the Son of God. In this instance, during the conversation at Solomon's Colonnade at the Feast of Dedication, Jesus made a miraculous escape to avoid death. The verses make it clear that He was surrounded, cornered by people already carrying their weapons of choice. But when they tried to grab Him, He managed to slip away.

God wouldn't let them touch His Son until exactly the right time—when everything was prepped and ready, and all the pieces had fallen together in the way He wanted them to so every prophecy would be fulfilled. Jesus died on the cross only because He chose it and God allowed it.

God's timing is perfect. Yet, to us, it can feel frustrating. At times, it can seem like things are taking too long; other times, it seems like they're coming on too fast. But we are always in the perfect spot for God's work when we're listening to and following Him.

WHERE ARE YOU?

What does God's timing in Jesus's life mean to you in your spiritual journey?

_____

_____

_____

_____

_____

Do you have any examples of God's timing demonstrated clearly in your life?

_____

_____

_____

_____

_____

Is there anything you feel like you're waiting on? How are you doing on trusting that He's in control?

_____

_____

_____

_____

_____

A PRAYER

God, Your timing is perfect. Help me to listen to You and help me to be patient so You can use my life to spread Your love. When I start to doubt or worry, remind me that You are in control. Thank You for allowing Your Son to give His life for us, to pay off our debts. I am forever grateful. In Your name, amen.

DAY 38:
THE EFFORT OF TRUE CHANGE

SCRIPTURE READING

LUKE 13:22–30 (NLT)

Jesus went through the towns and villages, teaching as he went, always pressing on toward Jerusalem. Someone asked him, "Lord, will only a few be saved?"

He replied, "Work hard to enter the narrow door to God's Kingdom, for many will try to enter but will fail. When the master of the house has locked the door, it will be too late. You will stand outside knocking and pleading, 'Lord, open the door for us!' But he will reply, 'I don't know you or where you come from.' Then you will say, 'But we ate and drank with you, and you taught in our streets.' And he will reply, 'I tell you, I don't know you or where you come from. Get away from me, all you who do evil.'

"There will be weeping and gnashing of teeth, for you will see Abraham, Isaac, Jacob, and all the prophets in the Kingdom of God, but you will be thrown out. And people will come from all over the world—from east and west, north and south—to take their places in the Kingdom of God. And note this: Some who seem least important now will be the greatest then, and some who are the greatest now will be least important then."

LIFE LESSONS

Hanging out with Christians, being best friends with one, following a close set of adopted church rules, restricting yourself to "Christian culture," and doing church-related events—those things don't make someone a Christian. What we need is to have a genuine relationship with Jesus. If we don't, if we skip over that part entirely, we can still be involved with church activities, but we're not really following God. It's like hanging out in a workplace but never actually taking the job. That relationship with Jesus is what will drive our decisions, our purpose, our lives.

The phrase *"work hard"* (verse 24) is translated from a Greek word that means "make an endeavor" or "strive hard to receive something." Some people are simply not concerned enough to strive for their relationship with Christ. While no one can work hard enough to earn their salvation, Jesus here emphasized the effort needed to seek after God, to change our hearts to be like His. It takes commitment and intentionality to return to Him after every setback and to seek to glorify Him in our lives.

And, somberly, Jesus pointed out that once the door of opportunity closes, it will be too late. We can't keep waiting and watching on the sidelines and still expect a championship ring when all is said and done. If we never bother to join the team and participate in God's story, we will never know Him.

WHERE ARE YOU?

Are you watching from the outside or are you genuinely and actively getting to know God on a personal level?

_____

_____

_____

_____

_____

What do you find prevents you from seeking God more?

_____

_____

_____

_____

_____

The Bible clearly teaches that we are not saved by works. What is the balance, then, between what God has done for you and what work you have to put into your walk with Him?

_____

_____

_____

_____

_____

A PRAYER

God, please give me the endurance to keep striving after You, even when it's hard. Please help me to be an encouragement to others who are unsure—a source of hope, understanding, and wisdom. In Jesus's name, amen.

DAY 39:
UNWAVERING CONFIDENCE

SCRIPTURE READING

LUKE 13:31–35 (MSG)

Just then some Pharisees came up and said, "Run for your life! Herod's on the hunt. He's out to kill you!"

Jesus said, "Tell that fox that I've no time for him right now. Today and tomorrow I'm busy clearing out the demons and healing the sick; the third day I'm wrapping things up. Besides, it's not proper for a prophet to come to a bad end outside Jerusalem.

> *Jerusalem, Jerusalem, killer of prophets,*
>   *abuser of the messengers of God!*
> *How often I've longed to gather your children,*
>   *gather your children like a hen,*
> *Her brood safe under her wings—*
>   *but you refused and turned away!*
> *And now it's too late: You won't see me again*
>   *until the day you say,*
>   *'Blessed is he*
>   *who comes in*
>   *the name of God.'"*

LIFE LESSONS

As we have seen, you can't rush God's timing. You can try to force it, but it won't work. He is in control, and everything will happen in its rightful place at the proper time—the time He has set.

The Pharisees had already tried to arrest Jesus, but, as He said, His time had not yet come. So, they turned to scare tactics instead, hoping that Jesus would just run away in fear. Jesus wasn't even phased. Instead, He rattled off His to-do list—one that didn't currently include His death at Herod's hands. He had no fear because He knew the plan. They didn't.

Jesus was in complete control. He knew He would keep on doing what God called Him to do no matter what other people said. No matter how they tried to shake Him up or get rid of Him. He was there to accomplish His purpose and refused to be distracted or to waver from God's instructions. That's the kind of confidence in God that we should strive for: unwavering, unphased, and fully confident in His will.

WHERE ARE YOU?

What was the Pharisees' intention in warning Jesus of danger? What do you think they were hoping He would do?

How is Herod like a fox and Jesus like a hen protecting her chicks?

In what ways do people resist this kind of tender, protective care from God?

A PRAYER

God, I pray that You would strengthen my faith so that, like Jesus, I won't have to fear the threats of this world. Help me to trust You more. Your plan will prevail; help me to listen to You and follow Your will. Help me to trust in Your perfect timing and plan. In Jesus's name, amen.

DAY 40:
THE HARD QUESTIONS

SCRIPTURE READING

LUKE 14:1–6 (NIV)

One Sabbath, when Jesus went to eat in the house of a prominent Pharisee, he was being carefully watched. There in front of him was a man suffering from abnormal swelling of his body. Jesus asked the Pharisees and experts in the law, "Is it lawful to heal on the Sabbath or not?" But they remained silent. So taking hold of the man, he healed him and sent him on his way.

Then he asked them, "If one of you has a child or an ox that falls into a well on the Sabbath day, will you not immediately pull it out?" And they had nothing to say.

LIFE LESSONS

Ever had any unsettling moments where someone else outed you—even about something minor—and pointed out that your actions didn't line up with the standards you claimed to live by? Sometimes it's simply a helpful reminder to refocus and realign ourselves. Other times, it can be a harsh lesson that something is distinctly off in our lives.

In today's reading, it was the Sabbath day, Jesus was dining with a leading Pharisee, and the Bible notes that, as they were eating, "[Jesus] *was being carefully watched*" (verse 1). Now, the language of the New Testament here actually implies that people were looking at Jesus with malicious intent. Of course, Jesus always knows the motives of our hearts. So, when a sick man appeared, Jesus asked the people watching if the law permitted healing on the Sabbath. When they refused to answer (probably hoping He would do something wrong), Jesus healed the man right in front of them. But He didn't wait at all for them to react. He immediately followed up the healing with another question regarding what they would do if someone precious to them were hurt or suffering on the Sabbath. We all know the answer to that.

Jesus pointed out their hypocrisy directly. The first question they *would* not answer, and the second they *could* not answer. Jesus knew exactly what He was doing then, and He knows what He's doing now. Sometimes He will ask us questions that are hard for us to answer. Ones that point out something that isn't right or is hypocritical in our own lives. Take the time to really reflect when that happens. It's happening for a reason, and He's pointing out something that needs to change.

WHERE ARE YOU?

Are there any questions in your life that God is asking but you are refusing to answer?

_____
_____
_____
_____
_____

What is He trying to teach you?

_____
_____
_____
_____
_____

How can you trust Him with the questions you can't answer?

_____
_____
_____
_____
_____

A PRAYER

Jesus, open my heart to all You are teaching me. It can be hard to face up to certain areas in my life that I don't want anyone to see and that I don't want to acknowledge myself. Help me to answer You honestly, and give me the courage to admit my shortcomings so I can have an honest relationship with You and keep moving forward on my journey with You. In Your name, amen.

DAY 41:
POINTING AWAY FROM OURSELVES

SCRIPTURE READING

LUKE 14:7–11 (NIV)

When he noticed how the guests picked the places of honor at the table, he told them this parable: "When someone invites you to a wedding feast, do not take the place of honor, for a person more distinguished than you may have been invited. If so, the host who invited both of you will come and say to you, 'Give this person your seat.' Then, humiliated, you will have to take the least important place. But when you are invited, take the lowest place, so that when your host comes, he will say to you, 'Friend, move up to a better place.' Then you will be honored in the presence of all the other guests. For all those who exalt themselves will be humbled, and those who humble themselves will be exalted."

LIFE LESSONS

We live in an ultra-competitive society that constantly strives for first-place accolades. People dedicate their entire lives to winning at all costs, to being recognized, to becoming someone notable. For most people, it's not how you play the game, it's whether you win or lose, whether you make it to the top or not. Many people will give up everything and do whatever it takes for the win.

Jesus knew this about human nature. He knew we reserve seats of honor in social settings. He knew the recognition those who do well can earn. But He encouraged His followers to do the opposite of what the world does, in both our spiritual lives and our lives in general. Jesus said to take the attention off of ourselves and put it on Him. To lift up others, to encourage others, to love. And to see others as worthy. Paul would later emphasize the same principle in Philippians 2:3–4: *"Don't be selfish; don't try to impress others. Be humble, thinking of others as better than yourselves. Don't look out only for your own interests, but take an interest in others, too"* (NLT).

Especially when it comes to our spiritual walk, we should be pointing people toward God in every way possible, and one of the simplest ways to do this is in how we treat others. By lifting others up and making ourselves lesser, we make a bold statement for Christ. Then, when someone *does* recognize us and lift us up, how much better does it feel knowing that we did not seek or encourage that praise!

WHERE ARE YOU?

What does Jesus mean by encouraging us to take "the lowest place" (Luke 14:10 NIV)?

_____

_____

_____

_____

_____

How can we lift up others and think of them as better than ourselves? What does that mean to you?

_____

_____

_____

_____

_____

Read Philippians 2:5–11 and write down the characteristics this passage describes of the best servant: Jesus Christ.

_____

_____

_____

_____

_____

Write down specific ways you can imitate Jesus based on this passage.

_____

_____

_____

_____

_____

A PRAYER

Lord, forgive me for allowing my pride and competitive nature to affect the way I treat other people. Enable me to lift them up, to help them recognize their worth. Replace my pride and selfishness with Your heart for others. Don't let me look down on anyone. In Your name, amen.

DAY 42:
FOR THE GOOD OF OTHERS

SCRIPTURE READING

LUKE 14:12–14 (NIV)

Then Jesus said to his host, "When you give a luncheon or dinner, do not invite your friends, your brothers or sisters, your relatives, or your rich neighbors; if you do, they may invite you back and so you will be repaid. But when you give a banquet, invite the poor, the crippled, the lame, the blind, and you will be blessed. Although they cannot repay you, you will be repaid at the resurrection of the righteous."

LIFE LESSONS

Most of us, at some point in time, have found ourselves at the mercy of another person's ulterior motives. Maybe we were the friendly springboard for their new social circle or the unsuspecting tool for their recent promotion.

Yesterday, Jesus asked us to put others first. Today, He continues His teaching on humility by calling us to do things solely for the good of other people. Specifically, He calls us to act even when we know there is no immediate benefit for us whatsoever. He asks us to get rid of any kind of selfish motive when it comes to who we invite in or how we treat others.

If your motives are selfish, if you're looking for some kind of immediate reward (even if it's just attention), that is all you will get: a temporary moment of temporary reward. Something that probably won't last long even by earthly standards. When we do things selflessly, though, when we genuinely look to reach out to and care for people in unexpected ways and places, our actions take on a whole new effect. We are genuinely benefiting others in the long-term by adding to their lives, which is a reward in itself, and it changes our hearts too. There are eternal benefits for truly loving others without regard to what could be in it for us.

WHERE ARE YOU?

When was the last time you did something out of your comfort zone to help someone with entirely unselfish motives (not looking for anything in return at all)?

_____

_____

_____

_____

_____

Can you think of anyone in your life who would be considered less fortunate? How can you reach out to them in a positive way? What could you do for them?

_____

_____

_____

_____

_____

What are some beneficial things you could do in the lives of people in your community who couldn't repay you? As you answer, think about your gifts and what you bring to the world individually.

_____

_____

_____

_____

_____

A PRAYER

Jesus, I pray for a pure heart, that my heart would be more like Yours every day. Thank You for being a servant of God and the perfect example of humility. I pray for the people I don't notice who need help. Open my eyes so I can see them, and give me the wisdom to lift them up in a way that truly benefits them and not me. In Your name, amen.

DAY 43:
ACCEPT THE INVITATION!

SCRIPTURE READING

LUKE 14:15–24 (NIV)

When one of those at the table with him heard this, he said to Jesus, "Blessed is the one who will eat at the feast in the kingdom of God."

Jesus replied: "A certain man was preparing a great banquet and invited many guests. At the time of the banquet he sent his servant to tell those who had been invited, 'Come, for everything is now ready.'

"But they all alike began to make excuses. The first said, 'I have just bought a field, and I must go and see it. Please excuse me.'

"Another said, 'I have just bought five yoke of oxen, and I'm on my way to try them out. Please excuse me.'

"Still another said, 'I just got married, so I can't come.'

"The servant came back and reported this to his master. Then the owner of the house became angry and ordered his servant, 'Go out quickly into the streets and alleys of the town and bring in the poor, the crippled, the blind and the lame.'

"'Sir,' the servant said, 'what you ordered has been done, but there is still room.'

"Then the master told his servant, 'Go out to the roads and country lanes and compel them to come in, so that my house will be full. I tell you, not one of those who were invited will get a taste of my banquet.'"

LIFE LESSONS

It's easy to postpone the life that God intended for us. So often, we let our daily obligations or the expectations of others get in the way of our journey with Christ. We push off our time with Him for errands or for success, or we spend it being solemn and religious rather than enjoying it. Here God is, extending us an invitation for His banquet of salvation and hope, and some of us are turning it down.

Jesus gave three illustrations of excuses people made for not attending this magnificent feast. For some, their possessions were keeping them away from the banquet. For others, it was their jobs. For the final group, it was other people. Which of these areas is keeping you from experiencing His joy? From really diving in and *living*?

Everything is ready. We are invited to the feast! We have our invitation in hand. It's time we stop making excuses and accept! The world needs to see the joy that Jesus brings, and we need to be living *in* that joy. It's time to show up to the banquet and live it out. Nothing will compare to a life lived in the presence of God.

WHERE ARE YOU?

Do you think the people around you see and feel your sense of joy in Jesus? Why or why not?

What excuses are you making that might be keeping you from God's celebration?

What do you think it means for us that the master wants his house as full as possible no matter how far the servant must go to find people?

A PRAYER

God, help me to live out the truth that there is no joy like being with You. Help me to stop making excuses and start truly living right now. Give me the clarity to see what I need to change in my life or in my heart to start living joyously. In Jesus's name, amen.

DAY 44:
CLUED IN AND COMMITTED

SCRIPTURE READING

LUKE 14:25–33 (NLT)

A large crowd was following Jesus. He turned around and said to them, "If you want to be my disciple, you must, by comparison, hate everyone else—your father and mother, wife and children, brothers and sisters—yes, even your own life. Otherwise, you cannot be my disciple. And if you do not carry your own cross and follow me, you cannot be my disciple.

"But don't begin until you count the cost. For who would begin construction of a building without first calculating the cost to see if there is enough money to finish it? Otherwise, you might complete only the foundation before running out of money, and then everyone would laugh at you. They would say, 'There's the person who started that building and couldn't afford to finish it!'

"Or what king would go to war against another king without first sitting down with his counselors to discuss whether his army of 10,000 could defeat the 20,000 soldiers marching against him? And if he can't, he will send a delegation to discuss terms of peace while the enemy is still far away. So you cannot become my disciple without giving up everything you own."

LIFE LESSONS

Being a disciple, a follower of Christ, is not a journey where you can hide in the crowd. Jesus wants people who are committed. At some point, any non-committal lingerers will face the same choices as anyone else following Christ. They will be asked to make sacrifices of time or careers or friends.

Jesus wants people to fully know what to expect, what it takes to truly follow Him, and for them to choose Him anyway. He consistently makes sure everyone knows exactly what He is asking of them so they don't become prematurely burned out or misunderstand Him and lose out on the whole purpose behind being His disciple. In this passage, we see that Jesus weeded out the people who were following Him for the wrong reasons, people who might need to reevaluate their commitment.

Jesus wasn't looking for a crowd or for the largest possible following at any cost. He wanted genuine commitment that comes from truly understanding.

He wanted disciples. And that's what He still wants: people who will sacrifice their old lives for the hope He offers. Are you one of them?

WHERE ARE YOU?

Do you understand what it means to be ready to commit to Jesus in the long term? Write down any concerns or questions you still have about fully committing.

_____

_____

_____

_____

_____

Is there anything you think you might be holding on to that's preventing you from being completely committed?

_____

_____

_____

_____

_____

What does Jesus mean when He says, "And if you do not carry your own cross and follow me, you cannot be my disciple" (Luke 14:27 NLT)?

_____

_____

_____

_____

_____

A PRAYER

Jesus, help me to establish a solid foundation of understanding so I know what it means to truly follow You. I want to choose You and a relationship with You. In Your name, amen.

DAY 45:
AN UNDILUTED PURPOSE

SCRIPTURE READING

LUKE 14:34–35 (NIV)

"Salt is good, but if it loses its saltiness, how can it be made salty again? It is fit neither for the soil nor for the manure pile; it is thrown out.

"Whoever has ears to hear, let them hear."

LIFE LESSONS

By its very nature and character, salt is useful both as a preservative and for seasoning. But what does it mean for salt to "[lose] *its saltiness*"? Salt, in itself, without additives, is extremely stable. In biblical times, however, salt was often mixed with various compounds. When these compounds were exposed to humidity and other sources of moisture, sodium chloride would often be the first ingredient to dissolve—leaving behind everything but the sodium chloride itself. This rendered the powder useless in terms of seasoning or preservation. It was essentially no longer salt.

If we give in to worldly pressures, if we stop looking to Jesus and we compromise the basic nature and character of who God has called us to be, we lose our purpose, our saltiness. To continue representing Jesus and being the "salt" for the earth, we must maintain our purity of intent and our intensity of passion.

How pure are your motives and your passion for Jesus? Where are you getting your strength from? When life gets hard, what do you have left at the end of the day?

WHERE ARE YOU?

In your own words, how would you describe the salt and saltiness that Jesus is expecting of us?

_____

_____

_____

_____

_____

On a scale of one to ten, how salty do you think you are in terms of your representation of Jesus Christ to the world? Explain why.

_____

_____

_____

_____

_____

How are you keeping spiritual fervor alive in your life?

_____

_____

_____

_____

_____

A PRAYER

God, help me to keep my eyes focused on You and to be an example of Your nature and Your character. I pray for a pure heart with pure motives, fully intent on being like You and showing others who You are and what Your message means for the world. In Your name, amen.

DAY 46:
EACH AND EVERY ONE

SCRIPTURE READING

LUKE 15:1–7 (MSG)

By this time a lot of men and women of questionable reputation were hanging around Jesus, listening intently. The Pharisees and religion scholars were not pleased, not at all pleased. They growled, "He takes in sinners and eats meals with them, treating them like old friends." Their grumbling triggered this story.

"Suppose one of you had a hundred sheep and lost one. Wouldn't you leave the ninety-nine in the wilderness and go after the lost one until you found it? When found, you can be sure you would put it across your shoulders, rejoicing, and when you got home call in your friends and neighbors, saying, 'Celebrate with me! I've found my lost sheep!' Count on it—there's more joy in heaven over one sinner's rescued life than over ninety-nine good people in no need of rescue."

LIFE LESSONS

What do you suppose is God's favorite number? Some people might say His favorite number is seven because it symbolizes perfection. Others may say it is the number three because the Trinity is Three in One. But what about the number one?

In Luke 15, we find one lost sheep, one lost coin, and one lost son. Over and over, Jesus emphasizes that each individual, every single lost soul, matters to Him. He is always fighting for that one more. He is always searching out every single one of us. He is not satisfied until we are all with Him. He seeks after every soul that has strayed, and He celebrates when we return.

In a world that tends to determine success based on quantity, Jesus reminds us that we are not just part of a big group, a faceless number in the crowd. He is seeking out each of us individually. He wants every one of us to have our own individual relationship with Him.

WHERE ARE YOU?

What does this parable say about the way Jesus associated with lost and broken people?

_____

_____

_____

_____

_____

How valuable is one soul to Jesus?

_____

_____

_____

_____

_____

How has Jesus sought you out personally?

_____

_____

_____

_____

_____

A PRAYER

Dear Father, thank You for loving us and fighting for us as individuals. You seek us out personally and always fight for that one more. I am so thankful that You came looking for me and that You continue to call me when I'm lost. Thank You for Your healing and for the life You give. In Jesus's name, amen.

DAY 47:
NO LESS VALUABLE

SCRIPTURE READING

LUKE 15:8–10 (MSG)

"Or imagine a woman who has ten coins and loses one. Won't she light a lamp and scour the house, looking in every nook and cranny until she finds it? And when she finds it you can be sure she'll call her friends and neighbors: 'Celebrate with me! I found my lost coin!' Count on it—that's the kind of party God's angels throw every time one lost soul turns to God."

LIFE LESSONS

Have you ever lost something and then torn apart the whole house looking for it? It doesn't mean it's the only item of importance; it just means it is *that important* to you. If you had ten children and lost one of them in the grocery store, wouldn't you go looking for the one who was lost? Your efforts to find them wouldn't take away from the other children. The fact that you had nine other children wouldn't mean you felt like you had plenty already and could just leave the one behind. You would care for each of them.

That's how Jesus sees us. Every soul is valuable, and Jesus reiterates on several occasions that every soul is of equal value. No matter what we've done, the lengths we've gone to in messing up our lives, how many times we've turned to Him and then turned away—we are still valuable to Him and no less valuable for our brokenness.

Jesus will find us in our dark corners, wherever we've ended up.

WHERE ARE YOU?

Do you see all souls as being equally valuable, or do you think you might be carrying any preconceived biases that are affecting how you treat others? If so, what are they?

_____

_____

_____

_____

_____

How can you learn to see people as Jesus does?

_____

_____

_____

_____

Do you think the illustration of the woman lighting the lamp might have a greater meaning in regard to our own lives? How could you light a lamp to help out?

_____

_____

_____

_____

_____

A PRAYER

Jesus, help me to see other people the way You do. Help me to recognize the value in every single person. Please erase any competitive tendencies or pride from my spiritual life so I can meet all people on the same level and love them as much as I should. In Your name, amen.

DAY 48:
DESERVING OF THE SAME

SCRIPTURE READING
....

LUKE 15:11–32 (MSG)

Then he said, "There was once a man who had two sons. The younger said to his father, 'Father, I want right now what's coming to me.'

"So the father divided the property between them. It wasn't long before the younger son packed his bags and left for a distant country. There, undisciplined and dissipated, he wasted everything he had. After he had gone through all his money, there was a bad famine all through that country and he began to feel it. He signed on with a citizen there who assigned him to his fields to slop the pigs. He was so hungry he would have eaten the corn-cobs in the pig slop, but no one would give him any.

"That brought him to his senses. He said, 'All those farmhands working for my father sit down to three meals a day, and here I am starving to death. I'm going back to my father. I'll say to him, Father, I've sinned against God, I've sinned before you; I don't deserve to be called your son. Take me on as a hired hand.' He got right up and went home to his father."

"When he was still a long way off, his father saw him. His heart pounding, he ran out, embraced him, and kissed him. The son started his speech: 'Father, I've sinned against God, I've sinned before you; I don't deserve to be called your son ever again.'

"But the father wasn't listening. He was calling to the servants, 'Quick. Bring a clean set of clothes and dress him. Put the family ring on his finger and sandals on his feet. Then get a prize-winning heifer and roast it. We're going to feast! We're going to have a wonderful time! My son is here—given up for dead and now alive! Given up for lost and now found!' And they began to have a wonderful time.

"All this time his older son was out in the field. When the day's work was done he came in. As he approached the house, he heard the music and dancing. Calling over one of the houseboys, he asked what was going on. He told him, 'Your brother came home. Your father has ordered a feast—barbecued beef!—because he has him home safe and sound.'

"The older brother stomped off in an angry sulk and refused to join in. His father came out and tried to talk to him, but he wouldn't listen. The son said, 'Look how many years I've stayed here serving you, never giving you one moment of grief, but have you ever thrown a party for me and my friends? Then this son of yours who has thrown away your money on whores shows up and you go all out with a feast!'

"His father said, 'Son, you don't understand. You're with me all the time, and everything that is mine is yours—but this is a wonderful time, and we had to celebrate. This brother of yours was dead, and he's alive! He was lost, and he's found!'"

LIFE LESSONS

Jesus told the parables we've been reading the last few days to two distinct groups of people at the same time: *"By this time a lot of men and women of questionable reputation were hanging around Jesus, listening intently. The Pharisees and religion scholars were not pleased, not at all pleased. They growled, 'He takes in sinners and eats meals with them, treating them like old friends'"* (Luke 15:1–3 MSG). His audience was a mix of people: men and women with really bad reputations and the Pharisees and other religious teachers. These two groups represented those who were obviously on an unhealthy path and viewed poorly by society, and those who were on an un-redeeming path but failed to see it because they were doing so many things "right."

The first group can be identified with the wayward son in Jesus's parable. Even though the son was utterly lost in his selfishness, squandering what his father gave him, he repented and returned to his father's house. He learned from his mistakes and sought to redeem himself.

The second group can be identified with the older son, who refused to come to the party his father threw at his brother's return. The older son was lost in his external goodness, his self-proclaimed righteousness. He thought he deserved more, better, because he'd been doing the work and making better choices all along. Even though everything of his father's was already his, he was completely focused on himself and what he felt he deserved.

Both groups needed salvation, and both groups needed to let go of control and doing things their own way. Jesus came to reach all of us.

WHERE ARE YOU?

Are you more like the younger son or the older son? Explain your answer.

_____

_____

_____

_____

How is the father in this parable just like God our Father?

_____

_____

_____

_____

A PRAYER

Lord, thank You for seeking out the lost and giving everyone the opportunity to be saved. Please help me not to be judgmental or critical of other people; help me to remember that we are all in need of You. Help me to never look down on others. They deserve You just as much as I do. In Your name, amen.

DAY 49:
MANAGING THE "HOUSE"

SCRIPTURE READING

LUKE 16:1–13 (NIV)

Jesus told his disciples: "There was a rich man whose manager was accused of wasting his possessions. So he called him in and asked him, 'What is this I hear about you? Give an account of your management, because you cannot be manager any longer.'

"The manager said to himself, 'What shall I do now? My master is taking away my job. I'm not strong enough to dig, and I'm ashamed to beg—I know what I'll do so that, when I lose my job here, people will welcome me into their houses.'

"So he called in each one of his master's debtors. He asked the first, 'How much do you owe my master?'

"'Nine hundred gallons of olive oil,' he replied.

"The manager told him, 'Take your bill, sit down quickly, and make it four hundred and fifty.'

"Then he asked the second, 'And how much do you owe?'

"'A thousand bushels of wheat,' he replied.

"He told him, 'Take your bill and make it eight hundred.'

"The master commended the dishonest manager because he had acted shrewdly. For the people of this world are more shrewd in dealing with their own kind than are the people of the light. I tell you, use worldly wealth to gain friends for yourselves, so that when it is gone, you will be welcomed into eternal dwellings.

"Whoever can be trusted with very little can also be trusted with much, and whoever is dishonest with very little will also be dishonest with much. So if you have not been trustworthy in handling worldly wealth, who will trust you with true riches? And if you have not been trustworthy with someone else's property, who will give you property of your own?

"No one can serve two masters. Either you will hate the one and love the other, or you will be devoted to the one and despise the other. You cannot serve both God and money."

LIFE LESSONS

If someone asked you if you've managed your money and resources in the best way possible, would you be able to say yes? What about how you've spent your time and energy overall? If it seems like a worldly question, it's not. Jesus talked about money more than He talked about heaven and hell combined. In fact, He talked more about money than prayer. There are over five hundred verses in Scripture that deal with the subject of prayer, but there are over two thousand five hundred that focus on money.

The New Testament Greek word translated as *"manager"* ("steward" in some Bible versions) comes from two words that mean "a house manager." God calls us to manage His house, to manage what He gives us in this lifetime. He has blessed us with everything we have and calls us to be good stewards of it.

God holds us responsible for how we manage our time, talents, and treasures. In response, we need to be careful, resourceful, and faithful with what He's provided, keeping the long term in mind.

WHERE ARE YOU?

Why do you think Jesus spoke so often about money?

_____

_____

_____

_____

_____

How are you doing as a manager of everything God has given you?

_____

_____

_____

_____

_____

How are you currently being careful, resourceful, and faithful?

_____

_____

_____

_____

_____

A PRAYER

God, whether You bless us with a lot or a little, we want to thank You for what You've given us. Help me to be a better steward of everything in my life: my money, time, family, friends, connections, talents—all of it. Give me the wisdom to use it well. In Your name, amen.

DAY 50:
FACING OUR FAULTS

SCRIPTURE READING

LUKE 16:14–17 (NIV)

The Pharisees, who loved money, heard all this and were sneering at Jesus. He said to them, "You are the ones who justify yourselves in the eyes of others, but God knows your hearts. What people value highly is detestable in God's sight.

"The Law and the Prophets were proclaimed until John. Since that time, the good news of the kingdom of God is being preached, and everyone is forcing their way into it. It is easier for heaven and earth to disappear than for the least stroke of a pen to drop out of the Law."

LIFE LESSONS

Would you ever laugh in response to God asking you to give something up? The Pharisees would—and they did. When Jesus told the Pharisees that they couldn't serve both God and money, they didn't just let the comment slide. They sneered at Jesus! The Greek word translated here as *"sneering"* is found only one other place in the Bible: it is used in Luke 23:35 to describe the religious leaders scoffing at Jesus during His crucifixion. This word literally means "to turn up your nose."

The Pharisees *loved* money. They loved being rich more than they loved being kind or helpful or loving or patient. They loved money more than people... more than God. So, Jesus pointed out that money was their master, not God. Jesus equated this excessive love of money, this striving after it, wanting it more than anything, with a lack of love for God. The blatancy of this truth cut them deep. And they did not respond well.

It can be hard to have our faults pointed out to us, but we should never respond with contempt. We need to listen with an open heart and consider what's being said to us—just in case we are in the wrong. Otherwise, we don't give ourselves the option to change.

WHERE ARE YOU?

"What people value highly is detestable in God's sight" (*Luke 16:15 NIV*).
How are Jesus's words in this verse still true today?

_____

_____

_____

_____

_____

Is there anything Jesus is teaching that you're rejecting? Or anything you're hearing that's making you feel defensive?

_____

_____

_____

_____

_____

What does Jesus's final statement mean: "It is easier for heaven and earth to disappear than for the least stroke of a pen to drop out of the Law" (*Luke 16:17 NIV*)?

_____

_____

_____

_____

_____

A PRAYER

Jesus, thank You for finding ways to speak truth into our lives. Keep my heart and ears open so I can accept my faults with grace and take the right actions—ones that will bring about personal growth—rather than attempt to alter Your words into my own truth. In Your name, amen.

DAY 51:
TWISTED INTERPRETATIONS

SCRIPTURE READING

LUKE 16:18 (NIV)

"Anyone who divorces his wife and marries another woman commits adultery, and the man who marries a divorced woman commits adultery."

LIFE LESSONS

Have you ever tried to find a way around a rule you didn't like? People in biblical times did this too. They wanted to adjust God's message to fit their lifestyle rather than adjust their lifestyle to fit His Word. This twisting of His laws made loopholes for the more privileged in a situation while leaving others out in the cold. (Another form of greed, similar to hoarding money for money's sake.)

According to God's law, divorce necessitated a certificate for the woman, showing she was free to remarry. Otherwise, she was essentially abandoned. The law wouldn't allow her to remarry without it, and in such a patriarchal society, marriage was often a necessity. Although the law was initially meant to protect women so they could marry again and still be within the law, the Pharisees interpreted it to fit their own tastes, to mean that as long as they gave a divorce certificate, they were fine. Instead of treating their wives well or genuinely trying to love them, they ran through wives whenever they wanted. They took a law intended to protect people and flipped it into something that left others abandoned at the whim of greed.

WHERE ARE YOU?

In what ways have you been tempted to adjust God's Word to fit your lifestyle?

_____

_____

_____

_____

_____

How does this passage help you to see that God's laws are meant as a means of protection rather than as punishment or restriction?

_____

_____

_____

_____

_____

A PRAYER

God, help me to not be selfish. To treat others as kindly and graciously as I'd like to be treated, both in the small things and the large. Rather than looking at Your laws as restrictions on myself or ways to restrict others, help me to see how, through them, You protect us and our communities, inspiring love over exclusion or leaving anyone out in the cold. Help me to read Your laws with Your heart. In Jesus's name, amen.

DAY 52:
WHEN YOU'RE GIVEN MUCH

SCRIPTURE READING

LUKE 16:19–31 (NLT)

Jesus said, "There was a certain rich man who was splendidly clothed in purple and fine linen and who lived each day in luxury. At his gate lay a poor man named Lazarus who was covered with sores. As Lazarus lay there longing for scraps from the rich man's table, the dogs would come and lick his open sores.

"Finally, the poor man died and was carried by the angels to sit beside Abraham at the heavenly banquet. The rich man also died and was buried, and he went to the place of the dead. There, in torment, he saw Abraham in the far distance with Lazarus at his side.

"The rich man shouted, 'Father Abraham, have some pity! Send Lazarus over here to dip the tip of his finger in water and cool my tongue. I am in anguish in these flames.'

"But Abraham said to him, 'Son, remember that during your lifetime you had everything you wanted, and Lazarus had nothing. So now he is here being comforted, and you are in anguish. And besides, there is a great chasm separating us. No one can cross over to you from here, and no one can cross over to us from there.'

"Then the rich man said, 'Please, Father Abraham, at least send him to my father's home. For I have five brothers, and I want him to warn them so they don't end up in this place of torment.'

"But Abraham said, 'Moses and the prophets have warned them. Your brothers can read what they wrote.'

"The rich man replied, 'No, Father Abraham! But if someone is sent to them from the dead, then they will repent of their sins and turn to God.'

"But Abraham said, 'If they won't listen to Moses and the prophets, they won't be persuaded even if someone rises from the dead.'"

LIFE LESSONS

Note: People are divided over whether this story is a parable. Jesus doesn't introduce it as a parable, and its mention of specific names sets it apart from other parables. Whether this story is a parable or not, it continues the idea of stewardship and appropriately managing what we are given while here on earth.

Generosity to the poor isn't a new concept. In biblical times—perhaps even more so than today—it was expected that people with wealth would give to the poor. Doing so was considered virtuous. And just like today, people's motives for giving varied: while they could be acting out of true generosity, they could also be seeking to maintain their reputation.

The wealthy man in Jesus's story had everything. He was in a position that gave him the ability to help, but instead he blatantly neglected his role as a steward of resources. He chose money and extravagance over people. The rich man's selfishness spelled out his fate. When you're given much, you need to open your eyes and look around you. Being too self-involved can have the same effect as actively ignoring the pain and hardships of others.

The rich man and Lazarus are different in almost every way. However, Scripture says in Proverbs 22:2, "*The rich and the poor have this in common: the Lord made them both*" (NLT). Regardless of what we're given by God, we are in charge of using it effectively. God asks us to be aware of those around us and to ease their suffering if we can.

WHERE ARE YOU?

What does Proverbs 22:2 teach you about God?

How aware do you think you are of the people around you who are hurting?

_____

_____

_____

_____

_____

What are some easy ways to start helping these people or your community?

_____

_____

_____

_____

_____

A PRAYER

Jesus, thank You for watching over us. Help me to be more aware of my community and others around me who may be hurting or need help. Open my eyes to the situations where I have the resources to assist and support other people. And help me to encourage others to trust in You. In Your name, amen.

DAY 53:
LIGHTEN THE LOAD

SCRIPTURE READING

LUKE 17:1–2 (MSG)

He said to his disciples, "Hard trials and temptations are bound to come, but too bad for whoever brings them on! Better to wear a millstone necklace and take a swim with the fishes than give even one of these dear little ones a hard time!"

LIFE LESSONS

Our actions have consequences. In a world full of people who don't take their actions seriously, we need to be more self-aware and care about the well-being of those around us. Not only that, but we shouldn't be making life harder on others in general. That alone can put someone in a compromising situation. We should be lightening the load for people when we can, not pushing them down.

Today's Scripture documents the second time Jesus warned people of the danger of causing others to stumble. This could mean pulling them into an old addiction, encouraging bad behavior, otherwise putting them in a bad situation, or just plain discouraging them from a relationship with God.

We're to be light, not darkness—an example to others of God's love and hope, an encouragement to others when they are down. We need to take a good look at our lives and make sure we are drawing people *to* God, not pushing them away from Him.

WHERE ARE YOU?

Are there any areas of your life or attitude that might be pushing people away from God instead of drawing them to Him?

_____

_____

_____

_____

What kinds of things are stumbling blocks for you?

_____

_____

_____

_____

Do you feel that your life lightens the load or brings light to others? If so, in what ways?

_____

_____

_____

_____

A PRAYER

Jesus, I don't want to be the reason that others fall away or stay away from You. I want my actions to draw others toward You. Help me to be more aware of my actions and the way I live my life. Help me to be a light and an encouragement to others, bringing hope and lightening the weight of the world. In Your name, amen.

DAY 54:
FREQUENT AND FULL-ON FORGIVENESS

SCRIPTURE READING

LUKE 17:3–4 (MSG)

"Be alert. If you see your friend going wrong, correct him. If he responds, forgive him. Even if it's personal against you and repeated seven times through the day, and seven times he says, 'I'm sorry, I won't do it again,' forgive him."

LIFE LESSONS

Forgiveness without limits can be a hard principle to implement. However, it's not something we can set aside. Following Jesus isn't about accepting the easy commands and leaving out the difficult ones. We can't pick and choose.

Jesus instructs us to call someone in our community out if they're in the wrong and refuse to admit it—especially if their wrongdoing is hurting themselves or others. Being direct like this can be a challenge, but it can also lead to redemption. If the person recognizes their offenses, admits to them, and asks for forgiveness, we are to forgive them. Every. Single. Time.

Jesus rebuked sin while still loving the sinner. And He asks us to do the same. As long as the person is trying to change, we are to keep being there for them, supporting them, and not hold their previous actions against them. We are to give them unlimited opportunities to truly change, as God gives us the same.

WHERE ARE YOU?

List a few biblical examples of Jesus forgiving others.

How difficult is it for you to lovingly confront others in hopes of their repentance and restoration?

_____

_____

_____

_____

_____

What keeps you from extending forgiveness? What could you do to change that?

_____

_____

_____

_____

_____

A PRAYER

Jesus, help me not to shy away from the hard parts of my walk with You. Give me the strength to obey Your Word no matter how difficult it becomes. Help me to show the same kind of grace to others that You've shown me. In Your name, amen.

DAY 55:
A QUESTION OF MOTIVES

SCRIPTURE READING

LUKE 17:5–6 (MSG)

The apostles came up and said to the Master, "Give us more faith."

But the Master said, "You don't need more faith. There is no 'more' or 'less' in faith. If you have a bare kernel of faith, say the size of a poppy seed, you could say to this sycamore tree, 'Go jump in the lake,' and it would do it."

LIFE LESSONS

In today's Scripture passage, the disciples make a request that we all should be making of God: *"Give us more faith"* (verse 5). Jesus's answer initially seems surprising. How is it possible that we don't need more faith?! But we're missing the point. It's a question of our attitude and our motives.

What Jesus was really getting at was the motivation behind our requests for more faith. Do we want more faith because we want more of God? Or are we praying these words for selfish or faithless reasons? Are we asking because we're uncertain about God's existence in the first place? Or perhaps we just want to be a more notable Christian or want to appear better than our neighbor.

And here is yet another time when Jesus compares faith to a tiny seed. As He mentioned before, all it takes to do great things in faith is to just *have it*. God can do so much with just a little faith because it's actually about His power, not ours. Our little, tiny seed of faith is still enough for God to work in and through us in far-reaching ways. It's about opening ourselves up to God and whatever He may ask of us.

WHERE ARE YOU?

What does Jesus mean by "there is no 'more' or 'less' in faith" (Luke 17:6 MSG)?

_____

_____

_____

_____

_____

As you grow older in Christ, is your faith maturing? In what ways?

_____

_____

_____

_____

_____

How does someone grow their faith?

_____

_____

_____

_____

_____

A PRAYER

Jesus, You can do so much with so little. I pray that You would use what faith I have to do great things, but please also increase my faith. Show me how to trust in You more. In Your name, amen.

DAY 56:
REMAINING IN OUR RIGHTFUL ROLE

SCRIPTURE READING

LUKE 17:7–10 (MSG)

"Suppose one of you has a servant who comes in from plowing the field or tending the sheep. Would you take his coat, set the table, and say, 'Sit down and eat'? Wouldn't you be more likely to say, 'Prepare dinner; change your clothes and wait table for me until I've finished my coffee; then go to the kitchen and have your supper'? Does the servant get special thanks for doing what's expected of him? It's the same with you. When you've done everything expected of you, be matter-of-fact and say, 'The work is done. What we were told to do, we did.'"

LIFE LESSONS

As our faith grows, and we start to see ourselves changing the world around us, we need to keep in mind who deserves the recognition. Apparently, the same was true for Jesus's disciples. After telling His disciples what faith the size of a seed can do—and before any kind of spiritual pride could slip into their hearts—Jesus gave them an analogy to teach them the proper perspective to maintain in a relationship with Him.

No Middle Eastern master of that time would have allowed his servant to take priority over himself. Just because the servant worked hard didn't mean he had the authority to assume the same position at the table as his master at the end of the day. The servant would come in from a day's work and continue his role of being a servant.

Thus, when we exercise our faith and amazing things happen, we are to give God all the credit and *keep on serving Him*. It is our privilege to do so, and we must keep that in perspective.

WHERE ARE YOU?

In what ways have you drawn attention to yourself when it was God who empowered you to say or do something?

_____

_____

_____

_____

_____

How can we stay humble in our lives and respond to our successes and accomplishments with a servant's heart?

_____

_____

_____

_____

_____

A PRAYER

Lord Jesus, help me to serve You with the humble attitude of a servant. Help me to give You all the recognition when You're working in my life and never try to take credit for what only You can do. In Your name, amen.

DAY 57:
SOMETHING GREATER

SCRIPTURE READING
....

JOHN 11:1–16 (NLT)

A man named Lazarus was sick. He lived in Bethany with his sisters, Mary and Martha. This is the Mary who later poured the expensive perfume on the Lord's feet and wiped them with her hair. Her brother, Lazarus, was sick. So the two sisters sent a message to Jesus telling him, "Lord, your dear friend is very sick."

But when Jesus heard about it he said, "Lazarus's sickness will not end in death. No, it happened for the glory of God so that the Son of God will receive glory from this." So although Jesus loved Martha, Mary, and Lazarus, he stayed where he was for the next two days. Finally, he said to his disciples, "Let's go back to Judea."

But his disciples objected. "Rabbi," they said, "only a few days ago the people in Judea were trying to stone you. Are you going there again?"

Jesus replied, "There are twelve hours of daylight every day. During the day people can walk safely. They can see because they have the light of this world. But at night there is danger of stumbling because they have no light." Then he said, "Our friend Lazarus has fallen asleep, but now I will go and wake him up."

The disciples said, "Lord, if he is sleeping, he will soon get better!" They thought Jesus meant Lazarus was simply sleeping, but Jesus meant Lazarus had died.

So he told them plainly, "Lazarus is dead. And for your sakes, I'm glad I wasn't there, for now you will really believe. Come, let's go see him."

Thomas, nicknamed the Twin, said to his fellow disciples, "Let's go, too—and die with Jesus."

LIFE LESSONS
....

Jesus had a special relationship with the family of Mary, Martha, and Lazarus, and He met often in the home of these three siblings. But just because this home was special to Jesus didn't mean the family living there would escape the trials and struggles of life. Even when Lazarus became very ill, and the two sisters sent a message to Jesus, He didn't head to them right away. He made a point of staying where He was for two more days.

Jesus made it clear to His disciples that Lazarus would be okay. Then He informed them that Lazarus was dead, which doesn't sound okay at all! But death is not the end for us. And this would not be the end of Lazarus's earthly life either.

Even when things seem hopeless, the struggles we encounter may be an opportunity for God to work in us or show Himself to others. We're going to go through rough times regardless—no one is exempt—but God has a plan, and something greater than we imagined may come out of it.

WHERE ARE YOU?

Do you find yourself struggling to trust God when things aren't going well?

_____

_____

_____

_____

_____

How could you get God's perspective for the problems you are facing?

_____

_____

_____

_____

_____

What do you think Jesus meant by the following: "There are twelve hours of daylight every day. During the day people can walk safely. They can see because they have the light of this world. But at night there is danger of stumbling because they have no light" *(John 11:9–10 NLT)?*

_____

_____

_____

_____

_____

A PRAYER

Lord, I know that in this fallen world, I will experience hard times and tragedies. Thank You for walking with me through each part of life's journey. I pray that whatever happens, it influences others to be in awe of You, to turn to You and not turn away. In Your name, amen.

DAY 58:
DEALING WITH DELAYS

SCRIPTURE READING

JOHN 11:17–27 (CEV)

When Jesus got to Bethany, he found that Lazarus had already been in the tomb four days. Bethany was less than three kilometers from Jerusalem, and many people had come from the city to comfort Martha and Mary because their brother had died.

When Martha heard that Jesus had arrived, she went out to meet him, but Mary stayed in the house. Martha said to Jesus, "Lord, if you had been here, my brother would not have died. Yet even now I know that God will do anything you ask."

Jesus told her, "Your brother will live again!"

Martha answered, "I know he will be raised to life on the last day, when all the dead are raised."

Jesus then said, "I am the one who raises the dead to life! Everyone who has faith in me will live, even if they die. And everyone who lives because of faith in me will never really die. Do you believe this?"

"Yes, Lord!" she replied. "I believe you are the Christ, the Son of God. You are the one we hoped would come into the world."

LIFE LESSONS

The longer you follow God, the more you discover that even His delays are divine. Although tragedy hits all of us at some point, and although the waiting game can wear us down, we can choose how to respond. When we don't understand why God is seemingly delaying to act or not answering prayers in the way we hoped, we simply have to rest the situation in God's hands, trust Him, and seek out His comfort.

When Jesus finally got to Bethany, Lazarus had been dead for four days, and Martha's first comment was pretty pointed. She knew that Jesus could have saved Lazarus. "Why weren't You here?" she implored. In response, Jesus reminded her of who He is. He is the One who raises the dead. He is the One who gives life.

We may not always get the answer we want from God, but when it seems like we're not getting an answer at all, do we still have faith in His power? Do we still believe in Him, or do we automatically turn away from Him instead of toward Him?

WHERE ARE YOU?

How can we trust in God's power to deliver even when we encounter delays in our lives?

_____

_____

_____

_____

_____

How can we continue to trust in God even when we don't get the answer we wanted?

_____

_____

_____

_____

_____

A PRAYER

Jesus, thank You for being "the resurrection and the life." I believe You have power over death and sickness. I also believe You are the One who gifts me with every next breath. Thank You for sustaining me and watching over me in each moment. In Your name, amen.

DAY 59:
MOVED AND MOURNING ALONGSIDE US

SCRIPTURE READING

JOHN 11:28–37 (CEV)

After Martha said this, she went and privately said to her sister Mary, "The Teacher is here, and he wants to see you." As soon as Mary heard this, she got up and went out to Jesus. He was still outside the village where Martha had gone to meet him. Many people had come to comfort Mary, and when they saw her quickly leave the house, they thought she was going out to the tomb to cry. So they followed her.

Mary went to where Jesus was. Then as soon as she saw him, she knelt at his feet and said, "Lord, if you had been here, my brother would not have died."

When Jesus saw that Mary and the people with her were crying, he was terribly upset and asked, "Where have you put his body?"

They replied, "Lord, come and you will see."

Jesus started crying, and the people said, "See how much he loved Lazarus."

Some of them said, "He gives sight to the blind. Why couldn't he have kept Lazarus from dying?"

LIFE LESSONS

Everything we read in the New Testament happened so long ago, and in such a different era, that sometimes when we read about Jesus, He can feel distant and unknowable. With Him being so powerful, and His teachings so intense, we can struggle to remember that He was a human man. Today's Scripture reading gives us a renewed sense of His humanity.

Now, it's Mary's turn to question Jesus. She said the same thing to Him that Martha had minutes earlier: *"Lord, if You had been here, my brother would not have died"* (verse 32). Scripture tells us that, when Jesus saw Mary weeping and the other people mourning, *"he was terribly upset"* (verse 33) and began to cry. Jesus was so concerned and moved because of their pain that He couldn't hold in His emotions.

Many of the deities people worshipped at that time were believed to rule at their own whims, without much regard for human feelings. But Jesus is compassionate and deeply cares for us. We are in the hands of a Savior who is moved by the hearts of His people and mourns alongside us.

WHERE ARE YOU?

God knows everything about you, and He always cares. How does His heart for you impact your heart for Him?

_____

_____

_____

_____

_____

How does it feel knowing Jesus weeps alongside you when you mourn or are sad?

_____

_____

_____

_____

_____

A PRAYER

Jesus, thank You for being a compassionate God, full of grace and mercy. You know every detail of my life and my heart, and You love me endlessly and completely just the same. Thank You for caring about the details, about my feelings and my pain. Thank You for holding me and comforting me. In Your name, amen.

DAY 60:
BRINGING US BACK TO LIFE

SCRIPTURE READING

JOHN 11:38–46 (CEV)

Jesus was still terribly upset. So he went to the tomb, which was a cave with a stone rolled against the entrance. Then he told the people to roll the stone away. But Martha said, "Lord, you know that Lazarus has been dead four days, and there will be a bad smell."

Jesus replied, "Didn't I tell you that if you had faith, you would see the glory of God?"

After the stone had been rolled aside, Jesus looked up toward heaven and prayed, "Father, I thank you for answering my prayer. I know that you always answer my prayers. But I said this, so the people here would believe you sent me."

When Jesus had finished praying, he shouted, "Lazarus, come out!" The man who had been dead came out. His hands and feet were wrapped with strips of burial cloth, and a cloth covered his face.

Jesus then told the people, "Untie him and let him go."

Many of the people who had come to visit Mary saw the things Jesus did, and they put their faith in him. Others went to the Pharisees and told what Jesus had done.

LIFE LESSONS

During our faith journeys, many of us have struggled with periods of doubt or uncertainty, or feelings of being unworthy. At such times, we might hesitate to draw close to God again. Today's reading reminds us that, even if we've doubted or walked away, even if we've been gone for a while and feel too damaged, or even if we're showing up committed every day and still feeling hopeless and beaten down by the world, Jesus can bring us new life.

If Lazarus could be dead for four days and still be brought back to life, Jesus is more than capable of giving life to you as well. Everyone present at the tomb thought Lazarus was too far gone. Jesus knew their doubts well enough that He made a point of spelling out His prayer to God in front of them so they would connect the miracle with Him and note the link to His Father.

No matter how deep the pit of despair you're in, how heavy the world might feel, or what you've experienced or done, Jesus is here, waiting, ready to walk you out of the dark places. He has compassion for you and cares about what you've been through. He is always calling, ready to pull us into the light if we let Him.

WHERE ARE YOU?

How do the audible prayers of Jesus, made to ensure we hear them, impact your walk of faith?

_____

_____

_____

_____

In what ways can His prayers not only teach you about prayer, but also become your own prayers?

_____

_____

_____

_____

Is there any part of your heart that needs to be brought back to life? Do you or does any part of you still feel dead or dark? How will you trust Jesus to bring you new life?

_____

_____

_____

_____

A PRAYER

Jesus, You are more than capable of bringing life to what is dead. Please meet me in the parts of my heart that are struggling, dark, or lifeless. I want to live fully in every manner possible, open to You and Your plans for me. In Your name, amen.

DAY 61:
THE FINAL TURNING POINT

SCRIPTURE READING

JOHN 11:47–54 (CEV)

Then the chief priests and the Pharisees called the council together and said, "What should we do? This man is working a lot of miracles. If we don't stop him now, everyone will put their faith in him. Then the Romans will come and destroy our temple and our nation."

One of the council members was Caiaphas, who was also high priest that year. He spoke up and said, "You people don't have any sense at all! Don't you know it is better for one person to die for the people than for the whole nation to be destroyed?" Caiaphas did not say this on his own. As high priest that year, he was prophesying that Jesus would die for the nation. Yet Jesus would not die just for the Jewish nation. He would die to bring together all of God's scattered people. From that day on, the council started making plans to put Jesus to death.

Because of this plot against him, Jesus stopped going around in public. He went to the town of Ephraim, which was near the desert, and he stayed there with his disciples.

LIFE LESSONS

After Jesus raised Lazarus from the grave, the religious rulers knew that soon everyone would believe in Jesus. They would lose control over their people as everyone turned to Him. In their minds, if they didn't stop Him, their whole nation would be ruined. So, God led the high priest Caiaphas to prophesy—without his even realizing it. Note Caiaphas's words: *"Don't you know it is better for one person to die for the people than for the whole nation to be destroyed?"* (verse 50). This was the final turning point. From this moment on, the Jewish leaders would be planning to kill Jesus to "save" their nation, setting a course for God's plan to come to fruition. Jesus would soon die for the nation, but also for the sins of the whole world, saving the world from itself.

WHERE ARE YOU?

Why were the religious leaders upset about Jesus performing so many miracles?

_____

_____

_____

_____

_____

In what ways were Caiaphas's words in verse 50 prophetic?

_____

_____

_____

_____

_____

How does this show God's gently guiding hand?

_____

_____

_____

_____

_____

A PRAYER

God, it's incredible how Your hand guides us. Even when we don't realize it, Your will is always done. Thank You for caring about us and investing in each one of us and our stories so much. In Your name, amen.

DAY 62:
TAKE NOTICE

SCRIPTURE READING

LUKE 17:11–19 (NIV)

Now on his way to Jerusalem, Jesus traveled along the border between Samaria and Galilee. As he was going into a village, ten men who had leprosy met him. They stood at a distance and called out in a loud voice, "Jesus, Master, have pity on us!"

When he saw them, he said, "Go, show yourselves to the priests." And as they went, they were cleansed.

One of them, when he saw he was healed, came back, praising God in a loud voice. He threw himself at Jesus's feet and thanked him—and he was a Samaritan.

Jesus asked, "Were not all ten cleansed? Where are the other nine? Has no one returned to give praise to God except this foreigner?" Then he said to him, "Rise and go; your faith has made you well."

LIFE LESSONS

How much do we notice God and His work around us on a regular basis? Do we truly recognize His achievements and His influence, or do we glance over them? A huge aspect of worshipping God is recognizing His work in our lives.

In today's Scripture, we must pay careful attention to a brief line in verse 14: *"And as they went, they were cleansed."* The passage tells us that Jesus met ten men stricken with leprosy. They called out to Him, and He told them to go and show themselves to the priests. This would normally be part of the process of reentering society *after* a leper was cleansed. But these lepers weren't healed when Jesus told them to go—they had to trust in Him and His instructions and put in their own effort. This was a test of faith. God healed them *while* they were following His directions. As they were walking away, one man noticed he was healed, and he immediately ran straight back to personally thank Jesus. He recognized what Jesus had done for him. He was fully aware of Jesus's power and the truth of who He was.

We have to notice and recognize God's work in order to be fully aware of who He is. To understand His power, His wisdom, and the depths of His love, we need to regularly acknowledge what He has done and what He is doing in our lives. We need to be aware and truly see things for what they are. Then we can fully live in awe of God and thank Him for *everything* He's been doing in our lives.

WHERE ARE YOU?

Why didn't Jesus just heal these men on the spot? What does that say about healing in our own lives?

Are you noticing God's work in your life on a regular basis? How do you think being more aware could change your view of and relationship with God?

How thankful are you for all that God has done? In what ways are you returning to Him to praise Him?

A PRAYER

God, I am so thankful for all that You have done. Please open my eyes and increase my awareness of what You are doing. Help me to see and recognize Your involvement in my life and Your power in the world so I can truly stand in awe of You, know You more, and thank You properly. In Jesus's name, amen.

DAY 63:
A DIFFERENT KIND OF KINGDOM

SCRIPTURE READING

LUKE 17:20–37 (NIV)

Once, on being asked by the Pharisees when the kingdom of God would come, Jesus replied, "The coming of the kingdom of God is not something that can be observed, nor will people say, 'Here it is,' or 'There it is,' because the kingdom of God is in your midst."

Then he said to his disciples, "The time is coming when you will long to see one of the days of the Son of Man, but you will not see it. People will tell you, 'There he is!' or 'Here he is!' Do not go running off after them. For the Son of Man in his day will be like the lightning, which flashes and lights up the sky from one end to the other. But first he must suffer many things and be rejected by this generation.

"Just as it was in the days of Noah, so also will it be in the days of the Son of Man. People were eating, drinking, marrying and being given in marriage up to the day Noah entered the ark. Then the flood came and destroyed them all.

"It was the same in the days of Lot. People were eating and drinking, buying and selling, planting and building. But the day Lot left Sodom, fire and sulfur rained down from heaven and destroyed them all.

"It will be just like this on the day the Son of Man is revealed. On that day no one who is on the housetop, with possessions inside, should go down to get them. Likewise, no one in the field should go back for anything. Remember Lot's wife! Whoever tries to keep their life will lose it, and whoever loses their life will preserve it. I tell you, on that night two people will be in one bed; one will be taken and the other left. Two women will be grinding grain together; one will be taken and the other left."

"Where, Lord?" they asked.

He replied, "Where there is a dead body, there the vultures will gather."

LIFE LESSONS

The Pharisees were looking for the wrong kinds of signs. They wanted a political sign that the Jewish nation would overthrow their Roman oppressors. But the kingdom of God isn't defined by physical boundaries. It's within the hearts of its people, led by Jesus, their King. The sign the Pharisees needed was a Savior, but they were looking too hard for a physical kingdom, not the spiritual kingdom that was already starting to thrive around them.

Jesus's life on earth was the sign we all needed. And He's calling for us to be ready and to not cling too tightly to what we have here. Because however you're living on the day He shows up, the condition of your heart when He arrives is what really matters. Either your heart will be ready or it won't. Either you lived as though You knew He was coming any day...or you didn't.

WHERE ARE YOU?

How does our current society compare with the culture of Noah's day?

_____

_____

_____

_____

_____

What do you think the following statement means: "Whoever tries to keep their life will lose it, and whoever loses their life will preserve it" (Luke 17:33 NIV)?

_____

_____

_____

_____

_____

How can we live so that our hearts are ready for Jesus every single day?

_____

_____

_____

_____

_____

A PRAYER

Lord, help me to live with my heart ready at all times. I pray that, every day, my heart would be open, loving, kind, generous, and seeking after You. I pray that I would live my life to its fullest, recognizing that each day is a gift. In Your name, amen.

APPROACH WITH DETERMINATION

SCRIPTURE READING

LUKE 18:1–8 (CEV)

Jesus told his disciples a story about how they should keep on praying and never give up:

> *In a town there was once a judge who didn't fear God or care about people. In that same town there was a widow who kept going to the judge and saying, "Make sure that I get fair treatment in court."*
>
> *For a while the judge refused to do anything. Finally, he said to himself, "Even though I don't fear God or care about people, I will help this widow because she keeps on bothering me. If I don't help her, she will wear me out."*

The Lord said:

> *Think about what that crooked judge said. Won't God protect his chosen ones who pray to him day and night? Won't he be concerned for them? He will surely hurry and help them. But when the Son of Man comes, will he find on this earth anyone with faith?*

LIFE LESSONS

Do you tend to ask God for something once or twice and then let the idea drift off? Maybe you assumed the answer was no or that it didn't really matter to God in the grand scheme of things.

In today's passage, Jesus compares our prayers to God to a woman who has been dealing with an uncaring judge. In the parable of the persistent widow, the judge is known to be unjust, but the widow still gets the justice she deserves due to her own diligence. She is so persistent that she drives the judge crazy. We should all have the same tenacity, the same passion. Imagine what would happen with a fair judge—someone who wants to give us good things and wants justice to prevail—if we approached them with the same amount of determination.

God cares about us. Just because we don't hear from Him immediately does not mean nothing will happen. He wants us to also care enough in return to push for what we want and not just expect things to happen. We need to approach Him with the same level of determination day after day. He will respond in kind.

WHERE ARE YOU?

In your prayer life, do you find yourself giving up too quickly? What do you think that says about your faith in God's response?

_____

_____

_____

_____

_____

Is there anything you need to be more persistent about in your prayer life?

_____

_____

_____

_____

What do you think about the phrase "pray to him day and night" (Luke 18:7 CEV)? What would that look like?

_____

_____

_____

_____

A PRAYER

Jesus, help me to develop perseverance and determination in my prayer life. Thank You for protecting me and for listening to me at all hours of the day or night. I know You care more about me than I could ever imagine and that You are always there for me. In Your name, amen.

DAY 65:
NO MORE OR LESS DESERVING

SCRIPTURE READING

LUKE 18:9–14 (CEV)

Jesus told a story to some people who thought they were better than others and who looked down on everyone else:

> *Two men went into the temple to pray. One was a Pharisee and the other a tax collector. The Pharisee stood over by himself and prayed, "God, I thank you that I am not greedy, dishonest, and unfaithful in marriage like other people. And I am really glad that I am not like that tax collector over there. I go without eating for two days a week, and I give you one tenth of all I earn."*
>
> *The tax collector stood off at a distance and did not think he was good enough even to look up toward heaven. He was so sorry for what he had done that he pounded his chest and prayed, "God, have pity on me! I am such a sinner."*

Then Jesus said, "When the two men went home, it was the tax collector and not the Pharisee who was pleasing to God. If you put yourself above others, you will be put down. But if you humble yourself, you will be honored."

LIFE LESSONS

None of us is worthy of God's love and grace. Whether we've been showing up every day in prayer and doing our best to follow God's will for thirty years or just falling on our knees in realization of our need for Jesus today, God doesn't have favorites. He looks at the condition of our hearts.

Pharisees were often known for their outward religion and obedience to the law. The name *Pharisee* means "separated one." Many Pharisees prided themselves on their adherence to the rules and how they were separate and different from others. Conversely, there was no one more despised or hated in all of Israel than a tax collector. Tax collectors worked for Rome and were considered traitors and thieves by their own people. The Pharisee in the story was living a righteous life—he was doing all the right things and even going above and beyond—but his attitude was self-righteous, his prayer self-congratulatory.

Meanwhile, the tax collector, knowing he was too far gone and deserved nothing, threw himself on God's mercy.

With God, there is no room for competitive spirituality or looking down on others. We should be lifting others up and helping them, not judging them. We are all living on God's mercy all the time, and that is the attitude we need to keep.

WHERE ARE YOU?

In what ways is your prayer life like the Pharisee?

_____

_____

_____

_____

In what ways is your prayer life like the tax collector?

_____

_____

_____

_____

A PRAYER

Lord Jesus, I pray for humility. Your grace and mercy is what saves us, not ourselves. Teach me to not look down on others but to lift them up and think of them as You do. Give me a pure and honest heart. In Your name, amen.

DAY 66:
LOOKING FOR LOOPHOLES

SCRIPTURE READING

MATTHEW 19:1–9 (NLT)

When Jesus had finished saying these things, he left Galilee and went down to the region of Judea east of the Jordan River. Large crowds followed him there, and he healed their sick.

Some Pharisees came and tried to trap him with this question: "Should a man be allowed to divorce his wife for just any reason?"

"Haven't you read the Scriptures?" Jesus replied. "They record that from the beginning 'God made them male and female.' And he said, 'This explains why a man leaves his father and mother and is joined to his wife, and the two are united into one.' Since they are no longer two but one, let no one split apart what God has joined together."

"Then why did Moses say in the law that a man could give his wife a written notice of divorce and send her away?" they asked.

Jesus replied, "Moses permitted divorce only as a concession to your hard hearts, but it was not what God had originally intended. And I tell you this, whoever divorces his wife and marries someone else commits adultery—unless his wife has been unfaithful."

SEE ALSO: MARK 10:1–12

LIFE LESSONS

We put ourselves in a compromising situation whenever we ask the Lord what is "allowed." It usually means we're trying to find a loophole! Rather than asking God, "What is allowed?" we should be asking, "What does God ask of me?"

This question about divorce was asked during a time when divorce was permissible for just about any reason. In New Testament times, a burned dinner might be considered a valid reason for divorce, and perhaps that is why Jesus felt this topic needed to be addressed.

God wants us to lead the best lives possible. He wants to protect us from harm. Divorce and the events that lead up to it are generally painful for both those directly involved and the people around them. It can leave many people feeling broken or unworthy of love. We are meant to find fulfilling relationships with people we can share our lives with. What does God ask of us? To do our best. To give it everything we have instead of looking for easier routes when times get hard. (Giving it everything we have does not mean staying in a dangerous environment. If you are experiencing physical or emotional abuse in a relationship, you need to protect yourself, set boundaries, and consult a trained counselor right away.) Sometimes, things won't work out, but relationships have a much better chance of being successful when we aren't actively looking for loopholes or justifying our own harmful actions.

WHERE ARE YOU?

Why do so many people choose to look at what is "allowed" over what God asks of us?

_____

_____

_____

_____

_____

Do you find yourself looking for loopholes in some of God's teachings? Which ones have been hardest to take at face value?

_____

_____

_____

_____

_____

Do you invest time in reading scholarly interpretations of the Bible? How do you think doing so could help you to avoid biases from reading without historical and cultural context?

_____

_____

_____

_____

_____

A PRAYER

God, help me to understand Your words and the heart behind Your words. Please help me to find Your truths, not my own opinions. I know that Your laws are meant to protect me because You don't like seeing me in pain and You want the best for me. Help me to trust in that. In Jesus's name, amen.

DAY 67:
DOING IT WELL EITHER WAY

SCRIPTURE READING

MATTHEW 19:10–12 (MSG)

Jesus' disciples objected, "If those are the terms of marriage, we haven't got a chance. Why get married?"

But Jesus said, "Not everyone is mature enough to live a married life. It requires a certain aptitude and grace. Marriage isn't for everyone. Some, from birth seemingly, never give marriage a thought. Others never get asked—or accepted. And some decide not to get married for kingdom reasons. But if you're capable of growing into the largeness of marriage, do it."

LIFE LESSONS

Jesus is being very honest here about an important truth: marriage is difficult! When you put two sinners in the same house, you definitely don't get sainthood. And Jesus's standard for marriage was too high for some of His disciples to even want to try.

God has high expectations for married couples. In fact, He offered marriage as a biblical example of His love for His church. In Ephesians 5:32, Paul makes this statement in the context of marriage: *"This is a great mystery, but it is an illustration of the way Christ and the church are one"* (NLT). This isn't meant to make a successful marriage feel like an insurmountable goal. Rather, God has high hopes for the love, support, and commitment we can find in marital relationships when we put in the work.

Furthermore, not everyone is designed for marriage, which is important to recognize. God has a purpose and a plan for all people, including those who never get married. Whether you end up tying the knot with someone or remain single, honor what God asks of you for your role in the world. Live the best life you can wherever it leads you.

WHERE ARE YOU?

Jesus says you need a certain aptitude and grace for marriage. In your own words, what does that mean or look like to you?

_____

_____

_____

_____

_____

How can you honor God's standard for whatever life He has called you to?

_____

_____

_____

_____

_____

In what ways can you demonstrate to God that you trust His plan for your life?

_____

_____

_____

_____

_____

_____

A PRAYER

Jesus, You are all I need. Thank You for creating marriage as a way of illustrating the unity You have with Your church and the love You have for us. In all of my relationships, help me to be supportive, loving, and kind. And as life continues, help me to trust that Your plan is right and what's best for me, and to live it well. In Your name, amen.

DAY 68:
NOT A BOTHER BUT A BLESSING

SCRIPTURE READING

MATTHEW 19:13–15 (MSG)

One day children were brought to Jesus in the hope that he would lay hands on them and pray over them. The disciples shooed them off. But Jesus intervened: "Let the children alone, don't prevent them from coming to me. God's kingdom is made up of people like these." After laying hands on them, he left.

SEE ALSO: MARK 10:13–16; LUKE 18:15–17

LIFE LESSONS

Not everyone understands the blessing of children—even those who have kids of their own. For those of us who are parents, don't we sometimes get too busy for our children or treat them as if they are a bother to us? And have we all perhaps gotten frustrated with other people's kids at times and treated them poorly?

When the disciples tried to turn away children, Jesus insisted they let them through to Him. Maybe His disciples thought He was too busy for kids or that they were a nuisance to Him—which sounds crazy when you think about Jesus's love for *all* people, especially those without much of a voice. Jesus *wanted* to bless the children. He wanted to interact with them and made a point of doing so, saying, *"Let the children alone, don't prevent them from coming to me. God's kingdom is made up of people like these"* (verse 14). He then took time to place His hands on their heads and bless them individually.

The Son of the Creator of the universe wanted the children to know He cared. We should model Jesus's example in the way we treat children. Jesus wants us to value and appreciate children, even when we're busy and stressed.

WHERE ARE YOU?

Do you take time to encourage children?

_____

_____

_____

_____

_____

Do you treat children as a bother or as a blessing? In what ways? What does that say about your relationship with Christ?

_____

_____

_____

_____

_____

Discuss your understanding of Matthew 19:14: "God's kingdom is made up of people like these" (MSG).

_____

_____

_____

_____

_____

A PRAYER

Jesus, help me to welcome children like You welcomed them. Children are a gift from You, and their total dependence is a great example of how we come to You in faith. Please give me patience and kindness when I'm around them and help me to be an example of what Your love looks like. In Your name, amen.

DAY 69:
A LACK OF DESPERATION

SCRIPTURE READING

MATTHEW 19:16–22 (MSG)

Another day, a man stopped Jesus and asked, "Teacher, what good thing must I do to get eternal life?"

Jesus said, "Why do you question me about what's good? God is the One who is good. If you want to enter the life of God, just do what he tells you."

The man asked, "What in particular?"

Jesus said, "Don't murder, don't commit adultery, don't steal, don't lie, honor your father and mother, and love your neighbor as you do yourself."

The young man said, "I've done all that. What's left?"

"If you want to give it all you've got," Jesus replied, "go sell your possessions; give everything to the poor. All your wealth will then be in heaven. Then come follow me."

That was the last thing the young man expected to hear. And so, crestfallen, he walked away. He was holding on tight to a lot of things, and he couldn't bear to let go.

SEE ALSO: MARK 10:17–22; LUKE 18:18–23

LIFE LESSONS

This man who came to Jesus had everything the world had to offer, but he was still missing the peace of God and his purpose for life. When Jesus led him to the commandments of God, the man claimed he had obeyed all of them. What else could he be missing? Jesus told him to sell all his possessions and give them to the poor so that he could follow Him. The man couldn't do it. He couldn't do what God was asking of Him. He wanted God, but he loved his possessions more. The one thing he lacked was exactly what he needed: a desperation for God that superseded everything else in life. He was willing to miss eternity with God because he wouldn't lay down his idols and replace them with a relationship with Jesus.

Even when we try our hardest, our own versions of "goodness" will always be imperfect because we are imperfect. Asking which good things we need to do to be okay with God is asking the wrong question. It creates a list of external actions that may only be done to benefit oneself, though they may look "good" from the outside. God calls for a changed heart. He wants us to look at our motivations. Who or what are we doing this for? If we're looking for the "things to do," are we still really listening to Him as to what He wants for us in our individual lives? Most importantly, we should be doing what He asks of us and laying down whatever might be in the way of that.

WHERE ARE YOU?

Are there any idols in your life that would prevent you from being able to follow God if He asked you to put them down and leave them behind? If so, what are they?

_____

_____

_____

_____

_____

Although money was his idol, what do you think this man's motivations were when he questioned Jesus?

_____

_____

_____

_____

_____

How would you respond if God asked you to sell everything you owned?

_____

_____

_____

_____

_____

A PRAYER

God, nothing compares to You. Please forgive me for following various things in life instead of You. Help me to lay down anything that prevents me from doing what You ask of me. And please give me the strength to do so. In Jesus's name, amen.

DAY 70:
MISPLACED SECURITY

SCRIPTURE READING
....

MATTHEW 19:23–30 (MSG)

As he watched him go, Jesus told his disciples, "Do you have any idea how difficult it is for the rich to enter God's kingdom? Let me tell you, it's easier to gallop a camel through a needle's eye than for the rich to enter God's kingdom."

The disciples were staggered. "Then who has any chance at all?"

Jesus looked hard at them and said, "No chance at all if you think you can pull it off yourself. Every chance in the world if you trust God to do it."

Then Peter chimed in, "We left everything and followed you. What do we get out of it?"

Jesus replied, "Yes, you have followed me. In the re-creation of the world, when the Son of Man will rule gloriously, you who have followed me will also rule, starting with the twelve tribes of Israel. And not only you, but anyone who sacrifices home, family, fields—whatever—because of me will get it all back a hundred times over, not to mention the considerable bonus of eternal life. This is the Great Reversal: many of the first ending up last, and the last first."

SEE ALSO: MARK 10:23–31; LUKE 18:24–30

LIFE LESSONS
....

After reading this passage, before we panic about owning any possessions at all, let's look first at what Jesus did not say. He did *not* say that rich people couldn't be saved. Just because we have possessions does not mean we all need to immediately toss them to the nearest charity organization and sell our houses. God blesses us with comforts here on earth, and we should enjoy them and be thankful for them.

Instead, Jesus said it is *difficult* for rich people to get into heaven. It's difficult because so many wealthy people put their security in their stuff and their dependence on dollars. And it's hard to tear away from that sense of physical security, even though we know it's tenuous at best (we never know what'll happen that might take it away). In addition, rich people have so many earthly possessions and comforts that many of them are blinded to their need for God.

It is far easier for those of us who are poor or in need to be totally dependent on God for everything, to genuinely trust in Him to meet those needs. None of us can afford to let life's blessings keep us from trusting in and seeing our real need for God.

WHERE ARE YOU?

How can we continue to see our need for Jesus if we live in a society full of plenty?

_____
_____
_____
_____
_____

In what ways do you need to refocus on what money can't buy?

_____
_____
_____
_____
_____

What does Jesus mean when He says, "No chance at all if you think you can pull it off yourself. Every chance in the world if you trust God to do it" (Matthew 19:26 MSG)?

_____
_____
_____
_____
_____

A PRAYER

God, help me to see that everything I have is because of You. And help me to know and really understand that if the world can take it away, it's not worth distracting me from You. I want to be thankful for Your blessings but wise enough to continue acknowledging my constant need for You. In Jesus's name, amen.

DAY 71:
NO ROOM FOR RESENTMENT

SCRIPTURE READING

MATTHEW 20:1–16 (NLT)

"For the Kingdom of Heaven is like the landowner who went out early one morning to hire workers for his vineyard. He agreed to pay the normal daily wage and sent them out to work.

"At nine o'clock in the morning he was passing through the marketplace and saw some people standing around doing nothing. So he hired them, telling them he would pay them whatever was right at the end of the day. So they went to work in the vineyard. At noon and again at three o'clock he did the same thing.

"At five o'clock that afternoon he was in town again and saw some more people standing around. He asked them, 'Why haven't you been working today?'

"They replied, 'Because no one hired us.'

"The landowner told them, 'Then go out and join the others in my vineyard.'

"That evening he told the foreman to call the workers in and pay them, beginning with the last workers first. When those hired at five o'clock were paid, each received a full day's wage. When those hired first came to get their pay, they assumed they would receive more. But they, too, were paid a day's wage. When they received their pay, they protested to the owner, 'Those people worked only one hour, and yet you've paid them just as much as you paid us who worked all day in the scorching heat.'

"He answered one of them, 'Friend, I haven't been unfair! Didn't you agree to work all day for the usual wage? Take your money and go. I wanted to pay this last worker the same as you. Is it against the law for me to do what I want with my money? Should you be jealous because I am kind to others?'

"So those who are last now will be first then, and those who are first will be last."

LIFE LESSONS

It can be frustrating to look at what others have when we have less and we've been working so hard. We might get resentful watching this happen, maybe even angry at God because it seems so unfair. But keep in mind, we're all receivers. Unfair as it may appear to us, we are all living on God's generosity. This goes for talents, wealth, spiritual gifts, and salvation itself. It is absolutely up to Him. They are His gifts to give as He pleases.

In this parable, the men who worked all day were upset when they were paid the same amount as the ones who worked only an hour. Timing didn't matter; they received the same reward at the end.

We should never resent others for the gifts they receive, but we should also never resent anyone for being offered God's grace, even if they're sliding in at the very last minute. God's gift of salvation is more than any of us deserve. Blaming God for being generous to others is silly because He has also been generous to us. All we can do is learn to accept His gifts with gratitude and use them well.

WHERE ARE YOU?

What does God's goodness, grace, and generosity mean to you today?

_____

_____

_____

_____

_____

In what ways have you been jealous of God's grace or gifts to others? Why?

_____

_____

_____

_____

_____

How can you rejoice with others when they receive God's gift of salvation and start reaping the benefits of a personal relationship with Him?

_____

_____

_____

_____

_____

A PRAYER

God, help me to long for others to receive all that You have for them. Please take away my jealousy and give me a generous and loving heart. Your gifts are Yours to give as You will, and You have more than enough grace to go around. Thank You for being such a generous God. In Jesus's name, amen.

DAY 72:
MOVING UP

SCRIPTURE READING

MATTHEW 20:17–19 (MSG)

Jesus, now well on the way up to Jerusalem, took the Twelve off to the side of the road and said, "Listen to me carefully. We are on our way up to Jerusalem. When we get there, the Son of Man will be betrayed to the religious leaders and scholars. They will sentence him to death. They will then hand him over to the Romans for mockery and torture and crucifixion. On the third day he will be raised up alive."

SEE ALSO: MARK 10:32–34; LUKE 18:31–34

LIFE LESSONS

Scripture specifically says that Jesus went *"up"* to Jerusalem. That was certainly true geographically. No matter where you traveled from, to get to Jerusalem, you had to travel upward due to its elevation. And while Jesus was going up to Jerusalem geographically, He was also going up willingly. The nearer He got to Jerusalem, the closer He was to fulfilling God's plan.

At the same time, multitudes of people were journeying to Jerusalem from all directions to celebrate the Feast of Passover. They were carrying with them sacrificial lambs to be laid on the altar. As the Lamb of God, Jesus was on the way to Jerusalem to sacrifice His life for the sins of the world. The door to salvation opens on the hinge of Jesus's sacrificial death on the cross. He made His way up to Jerusalem to make a way for us to one day move up into the presence of God.

WHERE ARE YOU?

Are you moving up in your relationship with God? In what ways?

_____

_____

_____

_____

_____

How do you see God's love for you in Jesus's determination to get to Jerusalem despite knowing what was to come?

_____

_____

_____

_____

_____

A PRAYER

Jesus, thank You for following God's plan despite everything You had to go through. I can't imagine what it was like to knowingly walk so far toward Your own betrayal and suffering. Thank You for holding strong. I am so grateful for the sacrifice You made for me. In Your name, amen.

DAY 73:
THE OPPOSITE OF POWER

SCRIPTURE READING

MARK 10:35–45 (MSG)

James and John, Zebedee's sons, came up to him. "Teacher, we have something we want you to do for us."

"What is it? I'll see what I can do."

"Arrange it," they said, "so that we will be awarded the highest places of honor in your glory—one of us at your right, the other at your left."

Jesus said, "You have no idea what you're asking. Are you capable of drinking the cup I drink, of being baptized in the baptism I'm about to be plunged into?"

"Sure," they said. "Why not?"

Jesus said, "Come to think of it, you will drink the cup I drink, and be baptized in my baptism. But as to awarding places of honor, that's not my business. There are other arrangements for that."

When the other ten heard of this conversation, they lost their tempers with James and John. Jesus got them together to settle things down. "You've observed how god-less rulers throw their weight around," he said, "and when people get a little power how quickly it goes to their heads. It's not going to be that way with you. Whoever wants to be great must become a servant. Whoever wants to be first among you must be your slave. That is what the Son of Man has done: He came to serve, not to be served—and then to give away his life in exchange for many who are held hostage."

SEE ALSO: MATTHEW 20:20–28

LIFE LESSONS

Matthew 20:28 and Mark 10:45 both contain this monumentally significant statement from Jesus: *"For even the Son of Man came not to be served but to serve others and to give his life as a ransom for many"* (NLT). The word *"even"* reiterates who Jesus is (in case His humanity made us forget where He came from): He is the Son of God. He is God in the flesh! If anyone should have been served by others, it should have been Him. He left His throne room in glory to give His life as a payment for our sins.

Since our God is willing to serve sinful humanity, we should be willing to serve as well. Jesus emphasized His upcoming sacrifice as the ultimate example of sacrificial service, putting others ahead of even His own life. He set the pattern that His children are meant to follow. We should be seeking the opposite of power over others. It's not about setting ourselves over other people; it's about getting down from our own self-built thrones of selfishness and putting others first.

WHERE ARE YOU?

In what ways can you become more of a servant to other people in your daily life, serving them over yourself?

_____

_____

_____

_____

How can we continue to put others before ourselves even when we are given more power over them here on earth?

_____

_____

_____

_____

What did Jesus mean when He said, "But as to awarding places of honor, that's not my business. There are other arrangements for that" (Mark 10:40 MSG)?

_____

_____

_____

_____

_____

A PRAYER

Jesus, thank You for paying a debt You didn't owe because it was a debt I would never be able to pay. Help me to follow Your example and unselfishly serve others. Keep my mind and heart clear even when power is given to me. Help me to use it to serve other people instead of using it for my own benefit. In Your name, amen.

DAY 74:
DON'T FORGET TO ASK

SCRIPTURE READING

MARK 10:46–52 (MSG)

They spent some time in Jericho. As Jesus was leaving town, trailed by his disciples and a parade of people, a blind beggar by the name of Bartimaeus, son of Timaeus, was sitting alongside the road. When he heard that Jesus the Nazarene was passing by, he began to cry out, "Son of David, Jesus! Mercy, have mercy on me!" Many tried to hush him up, but he yelled all the louder, "Son of David! Mercy, have mercy on me!"

Jesus stopped in his tracks. "Call him over."

They called him. "It's your lucky day! Get up! He's calling you to come!" Throwing off his coat, he was on his feet at once and came to Jesus.

Jesus said, "What can I do for you?"

The blind man said, "Rabbi, I want to see."

"On your way," said Jesus. "Your faith has saved and healed you."

In that very instant he recovered his sight and followed Jesus down the road.

SEE ALSO: MATTHEW 20:29–34; LUKE 18:35–43

LIFE LESSONS

Jesus tells us over and over to make our requests known to God, to keep at it, to be determined in our prayer lives. But often we don't even stop to think about what we *really* need from Him. We even forget to ask for the wisdom to discern what we need.

As Jesus leaves Jericho, He asks an essential (and often overlooked) question. In other translations, His question to Bartimaeus is phrased as, *"What do you want me to do for you?"* (Mark 10:51 NLT, CEV, NIV). What a question! Could you answer it for yourself today? Have you even really stopped to consider it? Bartimaeus's biggest need was to see, and he told Jesus so. Jesus responded in kind, telling him that his faith had healed him. Bartimaeus couldn't see Jesus, but Jesus could see his faith. Also, Bartimaeus knew he had to *ask* in order to be healed.

How often we sit around waiting for something we never bothered to ask God for! He'll meet us at our point of need, but we have to be in communication with Him. So, what *do* you want Jesus to do for you? What is your biggest need? Do you know? It's a good day to reflect on what you truly need God's help with.

WHERE ARE YOU?

What do you need God's help with? What do you want Him to do for you?

_____

_____

_____

_____

_____

How often do you reflect on your journey as a whole to see where you are, how far you've come, and what might have changed? What needs in your life has God shown you during previous reflections?

_____

_____

_____

_____

_____

A PRAYER

Jesus, I pray for persistence in my prayer life, but I also pray for wisdom and discernment. I want to pray with intention so I can make requests according to Your will and grow in You. Thank You for always responding to us and for rewarding those who have faith in You. In Your name, amen.

DAY 75:
EMBRACING A CLEAN SLATE

SCRIPTURE READING

LUKE 19:1–10 (NIV)

Jesus entered Jericho and was passing through. A man was there by the name of Zacchaeus; he was a chief tax collector and was wealthy. He wanted to see who Jesus was, but because he was short he could not see over the crowd. So he ran ahead and climbed a sycamore-fig tree to see him, since Jesus was coming that way.

When Jesus reached the spot, he looked up and said to him, "Zacchaeus, come down immediately. I must stay at your house today." So he came down at once and welcomed him gladly.

All the people saw this and began to mutter, "He has gone to be the guest of a sinner."

But Zacchaeus stood up and said to the Lord, "Look, Lord! Here and now I give half of my possessions to the poor, and if I have cheated anybody out of anything, I will pay back four times the amount."

Jesus said to him, "Today salvation has come to this house, because this man, too, is a son of Abraham. For the Son of Man came to seek and to save the lost."

LIFE LESSONS

Zacchaeus's story is a well-known narrative from Scripture; many children even grew up singing about him and the tree he climbed to see Jesus. But it's a good story for adults to take note of as well.

Zacchaeus was the chief tax collector, which means he was the most hated man in town. Although he was short, he was anything but small when it came to his level of power. He'd become wealthy off of his dishonorable dealings using his position. In fact, the people referred to him as *"a notorious sinner"* (Luke 19:7 NLT). Somehow, he still recognized Jesus for who He was and did everything he could to see Him. In Jesus's presence, Zacchaeus repented of his wrongdoings and made a promise of fourfold restitution to all those he'd ever cheated. Ready to change his life and atone for the things he'd previously done, he sought a clear slate with everything he had.

What kind of energy are we investing in seeking God and putting Him and others first? We should be as ready as Zacchaeus was to look at our own hearts, as ready to change, and as ready to restore relationships with the people we've hurt. We should be prepared to run after God and drop whatever He asks at His feet. After all, it's not about where we started—it's about meeting God where we are now and being ready to change, giving up whatever He asks of us to follow Him.

WHERE ARE YOU?

Have you ever gone back to someone and offered to atone for something you did that hurt them? How difficult was it to face them, even knowing you had changed?

_____

_____

_____

_____

_____

If you paid back fourfold for the restitution of your mistakes, who would you have to pay back and how much would you have to pay?

_____

_____

_____

_____

_____

What does this story say about God's forgiveness?

_____

_____

_____

_____

_____

A PRAYER

Jesus, thank You for meeting us wherever we are in life, whatever state we're in, no matter what we've done. You have the power to wipe that slate clean. I pray that we would all be ready to change and turn our lives around as much as this man was. Help me to admit when I'm wrong, and give me the strength to restore the relationships that I need to. In Your name, amen.

DAY 76:
OUR BEST WITH WHAT WE HAVE

SCRIPTURE READING

LUKE 19:11–28 (NIV)

While they were listening to this, he went on to tell them a parable, because he was near Jerusalem and the people thought that the kingdom of God was going to appear at once. He said: "A man of noble birth went to a distant country to have himself appointed king and then to return. So he called ten of his servants and gave them ten minas. 'Put this money to work,' he said, 'until I come back.'

"But his subjects hated him and sent a delegation after him to say, 'We don't want this man to be our king.'

"He was made king, however, and returned home. Then he sent for the servants to whom he had given the money, in order to find out what they had gained with it.

"The first one came and said, 'Sir, your mina has earned ten more.'

"'Well done, my good servant!' his master replied. 'Because you have been trustworthy in a very small matter, take charge of ten cities.'

"The second came and said, 'Sir, your mina has earned five more.'

"His master answered, 'You take charge of five cities.'

"Then another servant came and said, 'Sir, here is your mina; I have kept it laid away in a piece of cloth. I was afraid of you, because you are a hard man. You take out what you did not put in and reap what you did not sow.'

"His master replied, 'I will judge you by your own words, you wicked servant! You knew, did you, that I am a hard man, taking out what I did not put in, and reaping what I did not sow? Why then didn't you put my money on deposit, so that when I came back, I could have collected it with interest?'

"Then he said to those standing by, 'Take his mina away from him and give it to the one who has ten minas.'

"'Sir,' they said, 'he already has ten!'

"He replied, 'I tell you that to everyone who has, more will be given, but as for the one who has nothing, even what they have will be taken away. But those enemies

of mine who did not want me to be king over them—bring them here and kill them in front of me.'"

After Jesus had said this, he went on ahead, going up to Jerusalem.

LIFE LESSONS

As Jesus neared Jerusalem, many people believed that His kingdom would begin right away. Jesus told the parable of the ten servants to correct this misunderstanding. He made it clear that there was still work to do before the time would come.

God gave each of us purposes, gifts, and other blessings, and we're meant to do something with all of it. We can't just hide ourselves away in hopes that we will never mess up or poorly use what we have been given. Yes, we will make mistakes and misuse what God has given us. But what's most important is that we put ourselves out there and do the best with what we have. When we invest in our gifts and use our resources wisely, God entrusts us with more because our actions prove that we can handle more and use it well. When we purposefully hoard our gifts and resources, not sharing them or using them for anything good, there's no reason for God to give us anything more. It's our job to take what God has given us and use it well.

Sometimes it's difficult or scary to put ourselves out there and genuinely try, but our gifts are meant to be shared. Like the master and his servants, Jesus is coming back one day and will hold us accountable for what we've done with all He has given us.

WHERE ARE YOU?

What are you doing right now to invest what God has entrusted to you?

Do you think one day you will hear God say, "Well done"? If so, why? If not, what steps do you need to take today to hear those words in the future?

_____

_____

_____

_____

_____

A PRAYER

Jesus, give me the courage to use what You have given me and the wisdom to invest it well. I want to hear You say, "Well done." Thank You for trusting me with Your gifts in the first place. In Your name, amen.

DAY 77:
THE FOCAL POINT

SCRIPTURE READING

JOHN 11:55–57 (CEV)

It was almost time for Passover. Many of the Jewish people who lived out in the country had come to Jerusalem to get themselves ready for the festival. They looked around for Jesus. Then when they were in the temple, they asked each other, "You don't think he will come here for Passover, do you?"

The chief priests and the Pharisees told the people to let them know if any of them saw Jesus. This is how they hoped to arrest him.

LIFE LESSONS

Passover is a celebration that dates back to the exodus. When the Israelites were under the thumb of Pharaoh in Egypt, families that painted a lamb's blood over the doorposts of their homes were saved from the final plague. As time passed, the Israelites continued to celebrate their salvation by God's hand—but the world's overall salvation wasn't complete. No earthly being or creature could save us all, eternally. Jesus came as God's spotless and sacrificial Lamb. And in our reading, we're coming up on the specific moment for which Jesus came to earth.

Jesus's final week before His crucifixion is the focal point of all the Gospels. One-third of both Matthew and Mark deal with those final seven days. One-fourth of Luke's gospel and almost half of John's gospel are spent describing them. Of the eighty-nine chapters in the four Gospels, twenty-nine of them speak to His final week. The central point of Jesus's life and ministry is His sacrifice on the cross.

WHERE ARE YOU?

What does the amount of biblical material on the last week of Jesus's life before His crucifixion say to you about the importance of the cross? How does this apply to your spiritual life?

Do you continue to celebrate your salvation? What do you think it looks like to continue celebrating your salvation?

A PRAYER

Jesus, You lived a perfect life on earth to sacrifice Yourself for us. Thank You so much for loving us that much. Thank You for choosing to endure the cross in order to save us. In Your name, amen.

DAY 78:
LIFE TRANSFORMED

SCRIPTURE READING

JOHN 12:1, 9–11 (NIV)

Six days before the Passover, Jesus came to Bethany, where Lazarus lived, whom Jesus had raised from the dead....

Meanwhile a large crowd of Jews found out that Jesus was there and came, not only because of him but also to see Lazarus, whom he had raised from the dead. So the chief priests made plans to kill Lazarus as well, for on account of him many of the Jews were going over to Jesus and believing in him.

LIFE LESSONS

Shortly before Passover began, Jesus went to Lazarus's home in Bethany. John records both the excitement of the people and the attitude of the religious leaders at this point in time. Tensions were high. The people wanted to see Jesus and Lazarus; the priests wanted to *kill* Jesus and Lazarus because Lazarus was living proof of the resurrection power of Jesus.

When people looked at Lazarus, they saw the transformation from death to life that only God can provide and the evidence of Jesus's power and His connection to God as His Son. When the enemies of Jesus saw Lazarus, they didn't see a miracle or proof of divine power. They only saw a threat to their domain.

Our lives should display that incredible transformation, that sense of new life, as well. Too many of us are walking around, still not fully living, not fully accepting God's restoration. Whether we're held back by fear, uncertainty, or an inability to commit, we are missing out on the vibrancy that comes with true renewal and transformation from the inside out.

WHERE ARE YOU?

Do you believe that when people look at you, they see the resurrection power of Jesus in your life? If so, in what way(s)? If not, how can you live in such a manner that your life does show it?

_____

_____

_____

_____

_____

How has God brought you spiritually back to life? How is it evident in the way you live now?

_____

_____

_____

_____

_____

A PRAYER

Jesus, I want my life to reflect You and what You are capable of. Please continue to change my heart and to renew all parts of me to reflect Your heart and Your power. Give me the perseverance to keep going when it feels like the world is against me. Help me to continue to see others as You do and to have hope even during those times. In Your name, amen.

DAY 79:
DOWN TO THE DETAILS

SCRIPTURE READING

LUKE 19:29–40 (MSG)

When he got near Bethphage and Bethany at the mountain called Olives, he sent off two of the disciples with instructions: "Go to the village across from you. As soon as you enter, you'll find a colt tethered, one that has never been ridden. Untie it and bring it. If anyone says anything, asks, 'What are you doing?' say, 'His Master needs him.'"

The two left and found it just as he said. As they were untying the colt, its owners said, "What are you doing untying the colt?"

They said, "His Master needs him."

They brought the colt to Jesus. Then, throwing their coats on its back, they helped Jesus get on. As he rode, the people gave him a grand welcome, throwing their coats on the street.

Right at the crest, where Mount Olives begins its descent, the whole crowd of disciples burst into enthusiastic praise over all the mighty works they had witnessed:

> *Blessed is he who comes,*
> *the king in God's name!*
> *All's well in heaven!*
> *Glory in the high places!*

Some Pharisees from the crowd told him, "Teacher, get your disciples under control!"

But he said, "If they kept quiet, the stones would do it for them, shouting praise."

SEE ALSO: MATTHEW 21:1–9; MARK 11:1–10; JOHN 12:12–19

LIFE LESSONS

From this point on in our journey, we will be walking with Jesus to the cross. Today, we finally come to His triumphal entry into Jerusalem. Jesus, Son of the Lord of Creation, deserved something magnificent like a white stallion to ride in on. Instead, He came humbly, riding a colt.

The choice of a colt, though, is both symbolic and prophetic. In biblical times, a man of peace would ride a colt rather than a mighty warhorse. You see, Jesus didn't come as a conquering warrior but as a suffering servant. His death on the cross would bring peace to all mankind and reconcile us to God. And the colt was a fulfillment of multiple prophecies from the Old Testament. For instance, both Genesis 49:10–11 and Zechariah 9:9 were fulfilled by the simple action of Jesus riding a colt. These prophecies shout to us, just as the people did, that Jesus is the promised Messiah.

Isn't it incredible how God comes through even in the seemingly small details of life? He knows His plans for each and every one of us, down to the very last details.

WHERE ARE YOU?

How have you witnessed God in the specific details of your life?

_____

_____

_____

_____

_____

How does the fulfillment of prophecy increase your faith in the promises of God?

_____

_____

_____

_____

_____

A PRAYER

Lord, thank You for being a promise-making, promise-keeping God. You know the details of my life and my future. You have a plan for me. Thank You for caring so much about me. In Your name, amen.

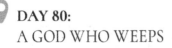

DAY 80:
A GOD WHO WEEPS

SCRIPTURE READING

LUKE 19:41–44 (MSG)

When the city came into view, he wept over it. "If you had only recognized this day, and everything that was good for you! But now it's too late. In the days ahead your enemies are going to bring up their heavy artillery and surround you, pressing in from every side. They'll smash you and your babies on the pavement. Not one stone will be left intact. All this because you didn't recognize and welcome God's personal visit."

LIFE LESSONS

Luke wrote that when Jesus came closer to Jerusalem and saw the city, He began to weep. With the Holy City in full view, Jesus broke out in tears of mourning for the souls of the people who failed to recognize Him.

Jesus mourned for Jerusalem on at least two occasions. Luke 13:34 records an earlier time in His ministry when He lamented over Jerusalem: *"O Jerusalem, Jerusalem, the city that kills the prophets and stones God's messengers! How often I have wanted to gather your children together as a hen protects her chicks beneath her wings, but you wouldn't let me"* (NLT). And here, Jesus cried when He saw Jerusalem during His triumphal entry. He was being celebrated and yet He wept for those who weren't ready for Him.

Jesus loves every single person with an undying, passionate love. He cries over those who choose not to turn their lives around, who encounter Him and choose not to see Him for who He really is. He weeps over those who miss their opportunity to be saved.

WHERE ARE YOU?

What does it mean to you that you have a God who weeps?

Does your heart ache for lost souls, for the broken and the hopeless and the selfish? What does your answer say about your heart for others? Does it reflect God's?

A PRAYER

Jesus, thank You for being a God who weeps for the souls of people, who wants us with You so badly. Please, make my heart like Yours. I want to care fiercely for others and their lives. Help me to be as welcoming and understanding as You are, even with people who make me uncomfortable or who are difficult. Let Your light shine out of me. In Your name, amen.

DAY 81:
SEEING HIM FOR WHO HE IS

SCRIPTURE READING

MATTHEW 21:10–11 (MSG)

As he made his entrance into Jerusalem, the whole city was shaken. Unnerved, people were asking, "What's going on here? Who is this?"

The parade crowd answered, "This is the prophet Jesus, the one from Nazareth in Galilee."

MARK 11:11 (MSG)

He entered Jerusalem, then entered the Temple. He looked around, taking it all in. But by now it was late, so he went back to Bethany with the Twelve.

LIFE LESSONS

Matthew's account reports that *"as [Jesus] made his entrance into Jerusalem, the whole city was shaken ["was in an uproar" NLT]"* (verse 10). They weren't in an uproar in the expectation that Jesus would soon be put to death. Or with the thought that He was about to suffer publicly and horribly. No, people were in an uproar because many believed Jesus was there to take charge and lead the Israelites out from under the Romans. Others thought of Him as another prophet of God, come to guide them into their future. The crowds were excited, and it was infectious—but it was also chaos because most of them were excited for the wrong reasons.

It should have been a clue to everyone that Jesus didn't arrive on a stallion, a warhorse, ready to take charge. But even though He was right there before them, people struggled in their understanding of who He was. Even those who saw Him as a prophet, recognizing His link to God, didn't see Him for who He fully was.

Many of us still don't see Jesus for who He really is, not fully, even though He's trying to tell us in so many ways. We still hold on to our opinions and pre-conceived ideas instead of listening and watching for Him to reveal Himself. The best way to get to know Jesus is to read His teachings, study His life and how He loved and lifted up other people, and begin trying to live and love like Him, begin the endeavor of being a servant to others. Jesus will be there for us every step of the way, whispering encouragement in our ears by the Holy Spirit.

WHERE ARE YOU?

What did you think of Jesus before you became a Christian?

_____

_____

_____

_____

_____

What do you think of Him now?

_____

_____

_____

_____

_____

List some steps you could take to get to know Jesus better.

_____

_____

_____

_____

_____

A PRAYER

Jesus, I pray that I would see You as You want me to, for who You really are in all Your power, glory, gentleness, strength—everything. It can be hard to wrap my mind around Your true nature, but I pray for more understanding. I want to genuinely appreciate all that You are. In Your name, amen.

MORE THAN LOOKING THE PART

SCRIPTURE READING

MATTHEW 21:18–19 (NIV)

Early in the morning, as Jesus was on his way back to the city, he was hungry. Seeing a fig tree by the road, he went up to it but found nothing on it except leaves. Then he said to it, "May you never bear fruit again!" Immediately the **tree** *withered.*

MARK 11:12–14 (MSG)

As they left Bethany the next day, he was hungry. Off in the distance he saw a fig tree in full leaf. He came up to it expecting to find something for breakfast, but found nothing but fig leaves. (It wasn't yet the season for figs.) He addressed the tree: "No one is going to eat fruit from you again—ever!" And his disciples overheard him.

LIFE LESSONS

As Jesus and His disciples were leaving Bethany, Jesus noticed a fig tree **full** of leaves but having no fruit. Mark mentioned that it wasn't even the **season** for fruit, but the hungry Jesus pronounced judgment on the fig tree. The **tree** immediately withered, never to produce figs again.

This passage can be confusing because, at first glance, it looks like an **angry** overreaction on Jesus's part. If it wasn't the season for fruit, why would **He** curse the tree? What we need to see here is that Jesus was illustrating a **parable** in action for His disciples.

One possible meaning of that parable alludes to the fact that the Scriptures generally depict Israel as a fig tree. Jesus's curse could be a symbolic **depiction** of the Jews who had rejected Jesus. It could also be an object lesson to **any** hypocritical "followers" of Christ: the fig tree appeared healthy and primed to produce fruit (or at least buds at this point in the season), but it **wasn't.** Figuratively speaking, the fig tree was pretending to be something that it **was** not. The leaves looked good for show, yet the tree was meant to produce **fruit** and should have had the early buds but didn't.

God expects us to produce fruit as well—to work at our relationship with Him—not just look the part.

WHERE ARE YOU?

Is your life bearing fruit, or is it nothing but leaves? Explain your answer.

_____

_____

_____

_____

_____

How could your life produce more fruit?

_____

_____

_____

_____

_____

A PRAYER

Jesus, I pray that my life will never be just an outward show. Help me to live a genuine life—one that influences other people for the better. I want to develop Your character and be a representation of Your love, hope, and generosity. In Your name, amen.

DAY 83:
A PLACE OF PRAYER AND WORSHIP

SCRIPTURE READING

MARK 11:15–19 (MSG)

They arrived at Jerusalem. Immediately on entering the Temple Jesus started throwing out everyone who had set up shop there, buying and selling. He kicked over the tables of the bankers and the stalls of the pigeon merchants. He didn't let anyone even carry a basket through the Temple. And then he taught them, quoting this text:

> *My house was designated a house of prayer for the nations;*
> *You've turned it into a hangout for thieves.*

The high priests and religion scholars heard what was going on and plotted how they might get rid of him. They panicked, for the entire crowd was carried away by his teaching.

At evening, Jesus and his disciples left the city.

SEE ALSO: MATTHEW 21:12–13; LUKE 19:45–48

LIFE LESSONS

In the beginning of Jesus's earthly ministry, Jesus, enraged by what He saw, fashioned a whip from some ropes and used it to clear merchants and money changers from the temple in Jerusalem. (See John 2:13–22.) Now, almost three years later, He found His house was still being corrupted by the religious leaders. What were His expectations for the temple?

The temple had been built so that people would have an opportunity to encounter the living God. Instead, people were merely encountering a religious market where money changers profited off of the temple's sacrificial system. Rather than finding a place to focus on worship or Scripture, attendees were distracted and angered by the unfair business transactions going on. Not the ideal experience for someone genuinely trying to worship God.

Jesus's words in Matthew 21:13 offer clarity as to what God wants His house to look like: *"The Scriptures declare, 'My Temple will be called a house of prayer,' but you have turned it into a den of thieves"* (NLT). God wants His house to be a place of prayer and worship. A place devoted to God. It is a haven for all people from all nations to come humbly and honestly before Him. And they should be able to do so without being cheated out of money—or prevented or distracted away from honoring God.

WHERE ARE YOU?

What are your thoughts on what Jesus said in Mark 11:17: "My house was designated a house of prayer for the nations; you've turned it into a hangout for thieves" (MSG)?

_____

_____

_____

_____

_____

Why is anger so often the response when sin is encountered?

_____

_____

_____

_____

_____

How can we ensure that people are finding safe spaces in which to encounter God?

_____

_____

_____

_____

_____

A PRAYER

Jesus, I don't want to approach Your houses of worship irreverently or ruin the experience of worship for other people. Help me to honor You in all that I do. Help me to contribute to making these spaces feel like places of worship, where people can come to both discover and spend time with You. In Your name, amen.

NO DOUBTS

SCRIPTURE READING

MARK 11:20–24 (NIV)

In the morning, as they went along, they saw the fig tree withered from the roots. Peter remembered and said to Jesus, "Rabbi, look! The fig tree you cursed has withered!"

"Have faith in God," Jesus answered. "Truly I tell you, if anyone says to this mountain, 'Go, throw yourself into the sea,' and does not doubt in their heart but believes that what they say will happen, it will be done for them. Therefore I tell you, whatever you ask for in prayer, believe that you have received it, and it will be yours."

SEE ALSO: MATTHEW 21:20–22

LIFE LESSONS

As Jesus and His disciples walked along, they passed the fig tree that Jesus had cursed the previous day. Mark mentions that *"they saw the fig tree withered from the roots"* (verse 20). In less than twenty-four hours, this fig tree had withered at its core, every bit of it. It didn't just have a dead leaf or two; the entire plant had died from its center.

From that visual illustration, Jesus told His disciples that they could have mountain-moving faith if they truly believed with no doubt in their hearts. But it's not about willing yourself to believe or using power just to prove your faith. You only find that kind of faith from walking closely with God. When your doubts are entirely erased, it means you're aligned with God and His will. You won't be walking around causing trees to wither or mountains to literally move. Rather, you'll be asking for things according to His will. When your heart is aligned with God's and you do what He asks of you, you will have no doubt concerning the incredible things He will do through you.

WHERE ARE YOU?

Do you find yourself doubting in your heart as you pray? Explain your answer.

_____

_____

_____

_____

_____

How can you more closely align your heart with God's to develop a greater faith?

_____

_____

_____

_____

_____

A PRAYER

Jesus, give me a heart aligned with Yours and mountain-moving faith. Help me to want what You want, pray Your prayers, and know You better. In Your name, amen.

DAY 85:
FORGIVE FIRST, FORGIVE NOW

SCRIPTURE READING

MARK 11:25–26 (NLT)

"But when you are praying, first forgive anyone you are holding a grudge against, so that your Father in heaven will forgive your sins, too. [But if you refuse to forgive, your Father in heaven will not forgive your sins.]"

Note: Some manuscripts add verse 26, shown in brackets.

LIFE LESSONS

"Forgive so that you can be forgiven" is an essential rule to live by. After all, we can't move forward in our walk with Christ if we're holding on to hurts, grudges, or bitterness. But it's also good to be the first to forgive. Don't wait to show the love and mercy of Jesus!

Mark is the shortest gospel. It is believed to have been written before Matthew, Luke, and John. It is fast-moving; in fact, one of its favorite words is a Greek term that means "immediately." By one count, it uses this word forty-one times. (To put this into perspective, this same word is used only twelve other times in the entire New Testament.)

Mark's approach stresses the importance of living out the Christian life *now*. Life moves quickly, and we only have so much time to fulfill our purpose in life and be an example to the people around us. Forgiven people should be the first to extend forgiveness.

WHERE ARE YOU?

What is your heart's response to what Jesus said in this passage?

_____

_____

_____

_____

_____

How can the urgency of Mark's gospel help you to let go of issues between you and others and forgive someone now?

_____

_____

_____

_____

_____

A PRAYER

Jesus, help me to forgive others immediately. I don't want bitterness taking root in my heart. Thank You for forgiving all my sins. Please give me the strength to forgive others. In Your name, amen.

DAY 86:
STUCK BETWEEN TWO FEARS

SCRIPTURE READING

MARK 11:27–33 (NIV)

They arrived again in Jerusalem, and while Jesus was walking in the temple courts, the chief priests, the teachers of the law and the elders came to him. "By what authority are you doing these things?" they asked. "And who gave you authority to do this?"

Jesus replied, "I will ask you one question. Answer me, and I will tell you by what authority I am doing these things. John's baptism—was it from heaven, or of human origin? Tell me!"

They discussed it among themselves and said, "If we say, 'From heaven,' he will ask, 'Then why didn't you believe him?' But if we say, 'Of human origin'..." (They feared the people, for everyone held that John really was a prophet.)

So they answered Jesus, "We don't know."

Jesus said, "Neither will I tell you by what authority I am doing these things."

SEE ALSO: MATTHEW 21:23–27; LUKE 20:1–8

LIFE LESSONS

The religious leaders were always trying to trap Jesus by His words. This was an impossible effort on their part because Jesus is the living Word and the master Teacher. When they questioned Him, He often turned their questions back on them. Their attempts to trap Him would always become their own trap, over and over. This was the case in our reading today.

The religious leaders wanted to know where Jesus got His authority, and Jesus turned around and asked them about the authority of John's baptism. Jesus had caught them either way they answered. If they said "heaven," then Jesus would ask them why they hadn't believed John. If they said "human," then the people listening would be angry because they all believed John was a prophet. The Pharisees couldn't answer the question. They were stuck between the fear of man and the fear of God. Jesus refused to answer their question because they were cowards, too afraid to admit their own wrongs even when those wrongs were pointed out to them so clearly.

Despite our best intentions, we all end up in situations where we become overly focused on what other people think, sometimes leading us to act in ways contrary to our own values or beliefs. Whenever you feel that discomfort, it's important to take a step back and try to give it an eternal perspective. Is their opinion worth leaving your values behind? Are you more worried about these short-term relationships or your eternal relationship with God?

WHERE ARE YOU?

Why do you think Jesus often responded to questions with questions of His own?

_____

_____

_____

_____

_____

Who do you fear the most: God or the people of this world? Why?

_____

_____

_____

_____

A PRAYER

Jesus, I believe You hold all authority and that You are who You say You are. Help me to listen to You and to obey Your words fully and faithfully. In Your name, amen.

DAY 87:
THE GREAT REVERSAL

SCRIPTURE READING

MATTHEW 21:28–32 (NIV)

"What do you think? There was a man who had two sons. He went to the first and said, 'Son, go and work today in the vineyard.'

"'I will not,' he answered, but later he changed his mind and went.

"Then the father went to the other son and said the same thing. He answered, 'I will, sir,' but he did not go.

"Which of the two did what his father wanted?"

"The first," they answered.

Jesus said to them, "Truly I tell you, the tax collectors and the prostitutes are entering the kingdom of God ahead of you. For John came to you to show you the way of righteousness, and you did not believe him, but the tax collectors and the prostitutes did. And even after you saw this, you did not repent and believe him."

LIFE LESSONS

Following Jesus isn't about saying the right words or putting on a nice show of obedience. You can stand there all day and tell everyone how obedient you are, and it will mean nothing if you don't actually do anything. It's about your follow-through. It's about turning around and obeying, even if you're a little late to the game.

Even though the prostitutes and tax collectors in today's passage initially rejected God, they ended up opening their hearts to Jesus and doing what He asked of them. In contrast, the religious leaders did not. They had all the show of following God without actually doing it.

In the parable, the first son seemed to be rebellious but proved to be righteous. The second son appeared to be righteous but was later shown to be rebellious. Much to their chagrin, Jesus was pointing out to the religious leaders that they were actually the rebellious ones. Meanwhile, the tax collectors and prosti-tutes who repented were the righteous ones.

These religious leaders thought they could trap Jesus with words and leave Him with no way out. Little did they know that if they nailed Jesus to a cross, He would save the world and draw all people to Himself. They didn't know that if you backed Jesus into a grave, He would make it grounds for resurrection. You can't trap Him.

WHERE ARE YOU?

How do you feel about the great reversal demonstrated in this parable?

_____

_____

_____

_____

Do you find yourself judging people based on who they are now, or do you imagine who they could be? Explain your response.

_____

_____

_____

_____

How can we continue making sure we're committed in our actions and not just making a show of obedience?

_____

_____

_____

_____

A PRAYER

Jesus, thank You for putting Your gift of salvation on level ground, so that it is not beyond anyone's reach. I pray that I would continue to follow up my words with actions. I also pray that I would be able to see people the way You do: imagine what they are capable of and see them for who they can be in You. In Your name, amen.

DAY 88:
THE UNMISSABLE STEP

SCRIPTURE READING
....

MARK 12:1–12 (MSG)

Then Jesus started telling them stories. "A man planted a vineyard. He fenced it, dug a winepress, erected a watchtower, turned it over to the farmhands, and went off on a trip. At the time for harvest, he sent a servant back to the farmhands to collect his profits.

"They grabbed him, beat him up, and sent him off empty-handed. So he sent another servant. That one they tarred and feathered. He sent another and that one they killed. And on and on, many others. Some they beat up, some they killed.

"Finally there was only one left: a beloved son. In a last-ditch effort, he sent him, thinking, 'Surely they will respect my son.'

"But those farmhands saw their chance. They rubbed their hands together in greed and said, 'This is the heir! Let's kill him and have it all for ourselves.' They grabbed him, killed him, and threw him over the fence.

"What do you think the owner of the vineyard will do? Right. He'll come and clean house. Then he'll assign the care of the vineyard to others. Read it for yourselves in Scripture:

> *That stone the masons threw out*
> *is now the cornerstone!*
> *This is God's work;*
> *we rub our eyes—we can hardly believe it!"*

They wanted to lynch him then and there but, intimidated by public opinion, held back. They knew the story was about them. They got away from there as fast as they could.

SEE ALSO: MATTHEW 21:33–46; LUKE 20:9–19

LIFE LESSONS

The vineyard owner sent his servants and then he sent his *own son*. He offered the farmhands multiple opportunities to make things right. The servants sent to talk with them portray all the prophets that God had sent. The son represents Jesus.

Jesus taught the parable of the tenants to reveal to the religious leaders how much they hated Him in their hearts, how they were rejecting the words of both the prophets and God's Son. He was letting them know what would happen as a result of their greed and the way they had rejected God's laws just to hold on to power.

The vineyard owner did everything he could for the vineyard and the people in it. Likewise, God has given us everything we need for salvation. He has been good to all of us. God has revealed Himself and His goodness, trying to reach out to people time and time again. He gives us so many opportunities. At some point, though, each of us has to make the decision to stop rejecting Jesus and embrace Him and the change He brings to our lives. This is still an unmissable step for allowing God to work through us. Even if we think we are in charge or in control, that is not the case. We are not running the show. All the power is in God's hands.

WHERE ARE YOU?

How good has God been to you? Take time to consider your response.

How can we respond to God's goodness and what He's done for us?

_____

_____

_____

_____

_____

What do you think Mark 12:9 means: "He'll come and clean house. Then he'll assign the care of the vineyard to others" (MSG)?

_____

_____

_____

_____

_____

A PRAYER

God, thank You for sending the prophets and Your Son. Thank You for giving us so many chances to follow You and come back to You. You are so good to us. I pray that greed and a desire for control would have no place in my heart. In Jesus's name, amen.

DAY 89:
JOINING THE PARTY

SCRIPTURE READING

MATTHEW 22:1–14 (NLT)

Jesus also told them other parables. He said, "The Kingdom of Heaven can be illustrated by the story of a king who prepared a great wedding feast for his son. When the banquet was ready, he sent his servants to notify those who were invited. But they all refused to come!

"So he sent other servants to tell them, 'The feast has been prepared. The bulls and fattened cattle have been killed, and everything is ready. Come to the banquet!' But the guests he had invited ignored them and went their own way, one to his farm, another to his business. Others seized his messengers and insulted them and killed them.

"The king was furious, and he sent out his army to destroy the murderers and burn their town. And he said to his servants, 'The wedding feast is ready, and the guests I invited aren't worthy of the honor. Now go out to the street corners and invite everyone you see.' So the servants brought in everyone they could find, good and bad alike, and the banquet hall was filled with guests.

"But when the king came in to meet the guests, he noticed a man who wasn't wearing the proper clothes for a wedding. 'Friend,' he asked, 'how is it that you are here without wedding clothes?' But the man had no reply. Then the king said to his aides, 'Bind his hands and feet and throw him into the outer darkness, where there will be weeping and gnashing of teeth.'

"For many are called, but few are chosen."

LIFE LESSONS

God has spared no expense for each and every one of us. He has gone to great lengths to reach out to us, prepare us to hear Him, and offer us hope and a future. We need to accept God's invitation.

Israel's religious leaders got the invitations. They even received a command to attend, to follow their Leader. Yet, they not only refused to come, but they also repeatedly rejected or killed off God's prophets—and now would refuse

God once again. According to the parable, not only did it mean they weren't attending the feast, but it meant their favored status was gone. Revoked.

Accepting God's invitation doesn't mean simply saying that we're coming and then not actually showing up; it means arriving at the doors and following the King's commands. Showing up at the party means legitimately joining in, not just accepting and then doing our own thing. And in order to accept God's invitation to heaven's feast, we must be dressed in His righteousness.

WHERE ARE YOU?

What are your thoughts on the parable of the feast?

_____

_____

_____

_____

_____

What does it mean to be properly attired for God's invitation? Why do you think the proper attire is referred to as "wedding clothes" (Matthew 22:12 NLT)?

_____

_____

_____

_____

_____

How can you go about getting yourself ready?

_____

_____

_____

_____

_____

A PRAYER

Jesus, help us to remember what You spoke to us through Paul in Galatians 3:27: *"All who have been united with Christ in baptism have put on Christ, like putting on new clothes"* (NLT). We want to accept the Father's invitation, properly attired, and we look forward to meeting You face-to-face someday. In Your name, amen.

DAY 90:
OPEN UP AND DIG IN

SCRIPTURE READING

MATTHEW 22:23–33 (MSG)

That same day, Sadducees approached him. This is the party that denies any possibility of resurrection. They asked, "Teacher, Moses said that if a man dies childless, his brother is obligated to marry his widow and father a child with her. Here's a case where there were seven brothers. The first brother married and died, leaving no child, and his wife passed to his brother. The second brother also left her childless, then the third—and on and on, all seven. Eventually the wife died. Now here's our question: At the resurrection, whose wife is she? She was a wife to each of them."

Jesus answered, "You're off base on two counts: You don't know what God said, and you don't know how God works. At the resurrection we're beyond marriage. As with the angels, all our ecstasies and intimacies then will be with God. And regarding your speculation on whether the dead are raised or not, don't you read your Bibles? The grammar is clear: God says, 'I am—not was—the God of Abraham, the God of Isaac, the God of Jacob.' The living God defines himself not as the God of dead men, but of the living." Hearing this exchange the crowd was much impressed.

SEE ALSO: MARK 12:18–27; LUKE 20:27–40

LIFE LESSONS

The Sadducees were a group in Jesus's day who focused primarily on just the first five books of the Bible and didn't believe in resurrection. When they asked questions to try to trap Jesus (concerning a resurrection they didn't even believe in), Jesus told them, *"You're off base on two counts: You don't know what God said, and you don't know how God works"* (verse 29). This is a problem for many of us today as well. When you are unaware of God's Word, you are absent of His power and knowledge.

We can only understand God if we actually seek Him out. Not everything will make sense immediately (if anything at all). Much of it will take time and then effort and probably more time. There are a lot of mysteries we won't understand for quite a while. What we do know is what's been written and handed down. What we can do is spend time in prayer and actively commit to loving others and being like Jesus in the world. If we want to know God, we have to open our Bibles and dig in.

The great news is that by completing this book, you have already done just that. Congratulations on digging in. Congratulations on your work so far on this journey through Jesus's life!

WHERE ARE YOU?

What are your thoughts on God's title "I Am the God of Abraham, Isaac, and Jacob" being tied to His eternal nature?

_____

_____

_____

_____

_____

How can our knowledge of God's Word affect the way we live our lives?

_____

_____

_____

_____

Is there anything about God or how God works that you'd like to know more about? Make a list. Now go out and research! Seek answers to the questions you have.

_____

_____

_____

_____

_____

A PRAYER

Jesus, I want to be a better student of Your Word, a better student of You. I don't want to miss Your strength and influence in my life as a result of not putting in the effort. I pray that You would make me more like You. Thank You for walking with me on this journey where I can learn more about You and Your life here on earth. In Your name, amen.

Amen. You did it! You just spent ninety days studying and reflecting on the way Jesus interacted with, loved, and served others. You might feel your heart pricked for those around you, or you may feel convicted about the ways that your life has become insulated and closed off to showing love and giving others the best of you (instead of the leftovers). Whatever your takeaway from this book, praise God for His voice in your life and for opening your eyes to the ways in which He is calling you into deeper love for and service of others.

If you'd like the journey to continue, look for the fourth and final book in the Life Along the Way Series, *Jesus in Us: Living Wholeheartedly the Life He Intends*, in which we look at what it means to go all in for Jesus and to put everything we've learned and studied thus far into practice.

Jesus is calling you to a life that is more beautiful and intentional than you can ever know. He is tapping you on the shoulder even now, saying, "Hey, let's go! Let's live out a life of love and service." The choice now is yours.

CONTRIBUTORS TO THE LIFE ALONG THE WAY SERIES BY JOURNEYWISE

JourneyWise began as the passion project of Dr. Shane Stanford, a Methodist minister and author, and Dr. Ronnie Kent, a board-certified pediatrician and behavioral health specialist. These men, whose Christ-centered friendship and fellowship began nearly forty years ago, wanted to create a platform that would allow leading Christian thinkers, teachers, pastors, and content creators to share insights that would enable people to find their identity in Christ. Its faith-based media network helps people from all walks of life sit at the feet of Jesus and receive life from His Word. JourneyWise is part of The Moore-West Center for Applied Theology, which aims to train laity in biblical literacy, theological dialogue, apologetics, and critical thinking, and in serving through applied theology. It was founded for the purpose of equipping and engaging others to "love Jesus and love like Jesus" in the world. The Life Along the Way Series was developed to help fulfill that mission.

CONTRIBUTORS:

Dr. Shane Stanford is the founder and CEO of The Moore-West Center for Applied Theology, as well as the president of JourneyWise, The Moore-West Center's faith-based media network. Along with pastoring congregations in Florida, North Carolina, Mississippi, and Tennessee for more than thirty years, Shane served as host of *The Methodist Hour* on TV and radio, reaching more than thirty million homes nationwide. He was awarded an honorary doctorate in divinity from Asbury Seminary, and he holds a master of divinity degree in theology and ethics from Duke University Divinity School. As an HIV-positive hemophiliac, he has spoken nationwide about AIDS awareness, including on CNN, *Good Morning America*, and Fox News. He and his wife, Pokey, have three daughters and live near Memphis.

Dr. Ronnie Kent recently retired after a forty-one-year practice as a medical doctor in Hattiesburg, Mississippi. He is a graduate of the University of Mississippi and the UM School of Medicine, has been teaching Bible classes in churches for decades, and is the father of three and grandfather of ten. He and his wife, Anne, have been married for forty-four years.

Dr. Ray Cummings has been pastoring churches for more than thirty years. A graduate of William Carey College and New Orleans Baptist Theological

Seminary, he has a doctorate in ministry with a specialization in church growth and evangelism, and he is the coauthor of The 41 Series devotionals. He and his wife, Amanda, have four children and live in Purvis, Mississippi.

Anthony Thaxton is an Emmy Award-winning filmmaker, television producer, and painter. He directed the acclaimed documentary *Walter Anderson: The Extraordinary Life and Art of the Islander*, directed projects with Morgan Freeman and Dolly Parton, and is the producer of *Palate to Palette* on public television. His photography has been featured on *Good Morning America*, CNN, and *Fox & Friends*, and his vibrant watercolors have been featured in books and on numerous television programs. He and his wife, Amy, live in Raymond, Mississippi.

Keelin MacGregor is a collaborative writer, editor, and avid circus artist based in the Pacific Northwest. Coauthor of Amazon #1 new release *Jane Doe #9: A "Surviving R. Kelly" Victim Speaks Out*, covering abuse victim Lizzette Martinez, her most recent collaborative work is *The Deadly Path: How Operation Fast & Furious and Bad Lawyers Armed Mexican Cartels* with government whistleblower and former ATF agent Pete Forcelli.

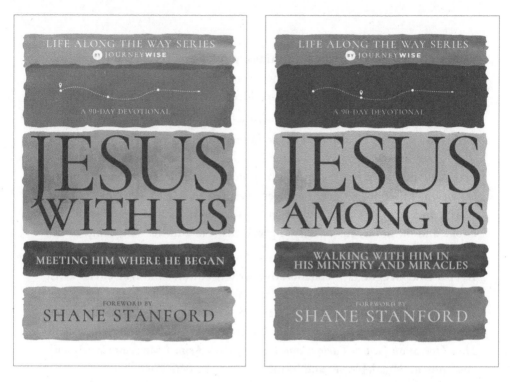

LIFE ALONG THE WAY SERIES

BY JOURNEYWISE

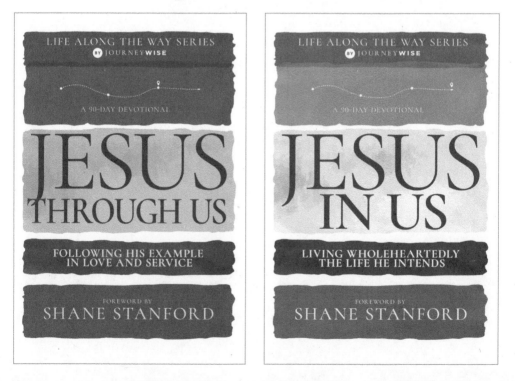